CHINA HANDBOOK SERIES

CULTURE

Compiled by
the *China Handbook* Editorial Committee
Translated by
Liang Liangxing and Zhu Peiyu

FOREIGN LANGUAGES PRESS   BEIJING

First Edition 1982

ISBN 0-8351-0991-7

Published by the Foreign Languages Press
24 Baiwanzhuang Road, Beijing, China

Printed by the Foreign Languages Printing House
19 West Chegongzhuang Road, Beijing, China

Distributed by China Publications Centre (Guoji Shudian)
P.O. Box 399, Beijing, China

Printed in the People's Republic of China

EDITOR'S NOTE

More than 30 years have elapsed since the birth of the People's Republic of China on October 1, 1949. "What is China really like today?" many people abroad wish to know. To answer this question, we plan to compile and publish a voluminous *China Handbook*, in which we intend to introduce the New China in every field of its activities. Emphasis will be on the process of development during the past three decades, the accomplishments, and the problems that still remain. The book will contain accurate statistics and related materials, all of which will be ready references for an interested reader.

To enhance the usefulness of the forthcoming volume, we plan to publish 10 major sections separately at first, so that we shall have an opportunity to take into consideration the opinions of our readers before all the composite parts are put together, revised and published as one volume. These separate sections are:

Geography
History
Politics
Economy
Education and Science
Literature and Art
Sports and Public Health
Culture
Life and Lifestyles

Tourism

Here, we wish particularly to point out the following:

First, the statistics listed in each separate book exclude those of Taiwan, unless otherwise indicated.

Second, the statistics are those compiled up to the end of 1980.

The *China Handbook* Editorial Committee

CONTENTS

Chapter One

NEWSPAPERS, BROADCASTING AND PUBLISHING

1. NEWS AGENCIES AND NEWSPAPERS

(1) NEWS AGENCIES

China has two news agencies. One is the state-owned Xinhua (New China) News Agency and the other is the privately owned China News Service.

The Xinhua News Agency The Xinhua News Agency has its origins in the *Red China News* Press, founded in November 1931 in Ruijin, Jiangxi. The present Xinhua News Agency was formally established on April 1, 1937 in Yan'an, and branch offices and sub-branches were established in some of the larger liberated areas after 1938. Initially, local newspaper offices had been responsible for sending news items and articles to Xinhua, but eventually Xinhua editorial branch offices were set up in combination with local newspaper offices. After May 1941, local news agencies were reorganized into Xinhua branches, which could independently set up direct contact with the Xinhua News Agency in Yan'an. The Xinhua News Agency was developing into a fair-sized news agency. It was releasing about 4,000 to 5,000 characters a day in domestic and world news, and transmitted reports from major news agencies at home and abroad. On September 1, 1944, it began overseas broadcasting in English. Towards the end of 1948, its first overseas branch was set up in Prague. In October 1949, after the founding of the People's Republic of China, the Xinhua News Agency became the nation's official news agency.

The head office of the Xinhua News Agency is located in Beijing. It consists of a general editorial office and editorial departments for domestic and international news, and a foreign news service. It also has professional departments for photography, foreign affairs and technology and also its own printing house and film processing workshop. It has branches in each of the 29 provinces, centrally administered municipalities and autonomous regions, and more than 700 reporters. Xinhua also runs a People's Liberation Army News Agency with 13 branches and more than 100 reporters. It also receives news from amateur correspondents in basic-level units throughout the country. In addition, it has branches in 85 foreign countries and regions, with over 150 correspondents. It also has branches in Hong Kong and the United Nations. Reports from correspondents and reporters within China are transmitted through its branches every day by telex, telegram and telephone to the head office in Beijing, and are uniformly released after processing by the domestic news editorial department. Xinhua branches abroad transmit news home mainly in English, French, Spanish and other languages; sometimes it also uses the Chinese phonetic alphabet or Chinese telegraphic code. The reports are sent by commercial telex or telegram in the countries where Chinese correspondents are stationed to Xinhua relay centres abroad, which in turn transmit the news to the head office in Beijing.

Xinhua's professional services are as follows: a. It provides news and newsphotos for domestic newspapers and broadcasting. Xinhua now releases about 40,000 to 50,000 characters daily in home and world news to Beijing's national newspapers and radio stations, about 30,000 to 40,000 characters to newspapers at the provincial, municipal and autonomous regional level, and about 10,000 to 20,000 characters to local papers below that level. b. Xinhua transmits domestic and world news abroad in English, Russian, French, Spanish and Arabic. The Chinese texts for these reports average about 10,000 to 30,000 characters daily. The news transmitted by Xinhua abroad includes items in English suitable for all countries, together with items in English, French, Spanish, Arabic and Russian specially designed for certain countries. c. Xinhua has news-gathering offices and professional contacts with many countries abroad. It has 25 offices in over a dozen countries and Hong Kong, from which it publishes and distributes daily and weekly bulletins containing telegraphic dispatches for foreign consumption. It also has contracts with news agencies in several dozen countries for the exchange of news and newsphotos without cost. More than 30 foreign news agencies now receive Xinhua news. d. It sends newsphotos abroad daily by radiophoto and by post. Xinhua can also provide special and feature articles at the request of domestic and foreign newspapers and journals. e. In Beijing, Xinhua issues a daily *News Bulletin* in Chinese, English, French, Spanish, Arabic and Russian, *Reference News* in Chinese and *News from Foreign Agencies and Press* in English and French.

The China News Service The main function of this agency is to supply news to overseas Chinese newspapers and journals. It was set up on October 1, 1952, as a private agency managed by a council of patriotic individuals with a wide range of backgrounds. The agency, which is located in Beijing, provides news items for Chinese language newspapers and journals abroad and in Hong Kong and Macao in the form of broadcasts, dispatches, news reports, feature articles and newsphotos. It also distributes abroad films on Chinese landscapes, art treasures, economic development and local opera.

The China News Service head office consists of departments for news, exclusives, photography, films and so on. It has branches in Guangdong, Fujian and Shanghai and an office in Hong Kong. Correspondents are also stationed in Yunnan and Guangxi.

(2) NEWSPAPERS

China's earliest newspapers The earliest newspaper in China was the *Dibao* (*Court Gazette*), distributed by an office (*di*) of the local government in the capital. Its major concern was with official items such as imperial edicts and memorials to the throne, and reports on the political situation. According to the latest research on historical records, the *Court Gazette* was already in existence during the reign of the Tang Emperor Xuanzong (r. 712-56), and continued in various forms down to the 20th century. Early in the 12th century, during the Song Dynasty, a hand-copied newspaper called the *Xiaobao* (*Small Paper*) was published. In 1638, during the reign of the Ming Emperor Chongzhen, the *Court Gazette* was printed from movable wooden types. Around the end of the Ming and beginning of the Qing Dynasty, the name was changed to *Jingbao* (*Peking Gazette*) and it became a commercial undertaking. It was a daily publication in the form of a small pamphlet. The printing was done from a clay plate coated with coal dust mixed with water on coarse paper, so the print was not very clear. In the late Qing, wooden and metal movable types were used in printing. Following the invasion of the colonialist powers, Western missionaries set up the first modern newspaper in China in August 1815. In the 50 years after the 1840 Opium War, foreigners set up over 300 newspapers, mostly in Chinese. They included the *Shanghai Xinbao* (*Shanghai News*), *Wanguo Gongbao* (*International Review*), *Shen Bao* (*Shanghai Gazette*), *Xinwen Bao* (*News Gazette*) and *Min Bao* (*Fujian News*). Most were published in Shanghai. The longest-running paper was the *Shanghai Gazette* (April 30, 1872 to May 1949), and the most important paper in the business world was the *News Gazette* (February 17, 1893 to May 1949). Both were founded by foreign businessmen, and after some time were taken over by Chinese capitalists. The earliest newspapers founded by the Chinese in modern times were the *Zhaowen Xinbao* (*Clarity News*) published in Hankou in 1873, and the *Xunhuan Ribao* (*Cycle Daily*) published in Hong Kong in 1874.

Progressive newspapers before Liberation The first newspaper run by Chinese bourgeois revolutionaries under the leadership of Sun Yat-sen was the *Zhongguo Ribao* (*China Daily*), founded in Hong Kong in January 1900. One of the most influential papers was *Min Bao* (*People's Journal*) founded in Tokyo in 1905 by the Tongmenghui (China Revolutionary League), an organization led by Sun Yat-sen; the first issue had a circulation of over 17,000. Another influential paper was the *Chinese Women's Paper*, founded in Shanghai by the famous revolutionary Qiu Jin. At the time of the May 4 Movement in 1919,

the development of the revolutionary movement encouraged the appearance of many progressive newspapers.
Some of the newspaper supplements in particular played
an important role in spreading bourgeois learning and
culture as part of the new cultural movement. The
supplement of the *Chen Bao* (*Morning Post*), *Juewu*
(*Awakening*), a supplement of *Minguo Ribao* (*Republic
Daily*), *Xue Deng* (*Academic Lamp*), the supplement of
Shishi Xinbao (*The China Times*) and the supplement of
the *Jing Bao* (*Peking Gazette*) were known as the "four
supplements of the new cultural movement". Another
influential journal was the *Tianjin Xuesheng Lianhehui-
bao* (*The Tianjin Student Union Bulletin*) edited by Zhou
Enlai, which showed an obvious tendency towards
socialism.

The Chinese Communist Party paid great attention to
the role of newspapers in the revolutionary cause. Soon
after the founding of the Chinese Communist Party and
during the First Revolutionary Civil War (1924-27), the
Communist Party founded newspapers in Beijing, Shanghai, Wuhan, Jinan, Guangzhou and other places. The most
influential were the *Laodong Zhoukan* (*Labour Weekly*)
in Shanghai and the *Gongren Zhoukan* (*Workers' Weekly*)
in Beijing. The *Labour Weekly* was an organ of the
Chinese Labour Union Secretariat, and was the first national newspaper for workers. It started publication in
the summer of 1921, and was banned on June 9, 1922 by
the Shanghai Municipal Council in the international settle-
ment for the "crimes" of publishing extremist opinions
and advocating labour revolution. The *Workers' Weekly*
was published in the name of the Workers' Weekly
Society by the Communist Party in Beijing. It started
publication in July 1921. In May 1922 the Chinese Labour

Union Secretariat moved to Beijing from Shanghai, and not long after, the *Workers' Weekly* replaced the *Labour Weekly* as the organ of the secretariat. In 1924, it became the journal of the Chinese National Federation of Railway Unions. It ceased publication in December 1925, with 133 issues behind it.

The central organ of the Chinese Communist Party during the Second Revolutionary Civil War (1927-37) was the *Hongqi Ribao* (*Red Flag Daily*). It began publication in Shanghai on August 15, 1930 and was forced to cease publication in March 1931.

On November 7, 1931, the Chinese Communist Party set up the Central Workers' and Peasants' Democratic Government in Ruijin, Jiangxi. A number of official newspapers were founded, including *Hongse Zhonghua* (*Red China*), *Douzheng* (*Struggle*), *Hongxing* (*Red Star*), *Qingnian Shihua* (*Young People's Truth*) and *Suqu Gongren* (*Soviet Area Worker*). The *Red China* subsequently became the combined organ of the Chinese Communist Party, the Central Workers' and Peasants' Democratic Government, the All-China Federation of Trade Unions and the Communist Youth League of China. This was the first fairly long-term newspaper printed in letterpress by the Chinese Communist Party in the revolutionary base areas. It published altogether 240 issues. In October 1934, it moved to north Shaanxi on the Long March with the Red Army. On January 29, 1937, it resumed publication in Yan'an, changing its title to *Xin Zhonghua Bao* (*New China Daily*). On May 15, 1941, it merged with the *Jinri Xinwen* (*News Today*), becoming a large-format paper under the name *Jiefang Ribao* (*Liberation Daily*). The *Liberation Daily* ceased publication on March 27, 1947, after 2,130 issues, when Yan'an was evacuated.

Other newspapers were also set up in liberated areas during the War of Resistance Against Japan (1937-45), including the *Jin-Cha-Ji Ribao* (*Shanxi-Qahar-Hebei Daily*), *Jizhong Daobao* (*Central Hebei Guide*), *Ji-Lu-Yu Ribao* (*Hebei-Shandong-Henan Daily*), *Dazhong Ribao* (*Popular Daily*), *Fuxiaobao* (*Daybreak*), *Kangzhan Ribao* (*Resistance Daily*) and *Jianghuai Ribao* (*Central China Daily*). The Communist Party's official newspaper in Kuomintang-controlled areas was *Xinhua Ribao* (*New China Daily*). It began publication on January 11, 1938, in Hankou and moved to Chongqing on October 25 the same year, where it circulated openly until banned by the Kuomintang government on February 28, 1947.

During the Third Revolutionary Civil War (1945-49), the newspapers continued to flourish in the liberated areas. One of the more important was the *Dongbei Ribao* (*Northeast Daily*) in the Northeastern China Liberated Area, which began publication on November 1, 1945.

Newspapers in China after Liberation The founding of New China greatly increased the number and circulation of newspapers. In 1950, the total annual circulation of national and provincial newspapers was 798 million copies; in 1980 it was 14,041 million copies, 17 times that in 1950. In 1980, there were 188 newspapers nationwide (not including local papers below the provincial level). New papers began to appear in 1980 and 1981, such as the *Zhongguo Nongmin Bao* (*Chinese Peasant Gazette*), *Zhongguo Fazhi Bao* (*Chinese Legal Gazette*) and the English-language *China Daily*. The publication of newspapers run by different organizations, trades, professions, regions, cities and counties was resumed or initiated, and evening newspapers also appeared.

The main national newspapers in China at present are listed below:

Renmin Ribao (*People's Daily*): Began publication on May 15, 1946, in Handan, Hebei, in the North China Liberated Area. After moving from Shijiazhuang to Beijing in January 1949, it became the organ of the Central Committee of the Chinese Communist Party in August the same year.

Guangming Ribao (*Enlightenment Daily*): Began publication in Beijing on June 16, 1949 as the organ of the Central Committee of the China Democratic League. At the end of 1952, it became the combined organ of the democratic parties. Its main readership now is composed of intellectuals.

Gongren Ribao (*Workers' Daily*): Organ of the All-China Federation of Trade Unions; began publication on July 15, 1949 in Beijing. Its main readers are workers, managerial personnel and trade union staff.

Zhongguo Nongmin Bao (*Chinese Peasant Gazette*): A comprehensive newspaper in simple language for peasants. It began publication in April 1980 in Beijing. It publishes two issues per week, with eight pages per issue.

Zhongguo Qingnian Bao (*Chinese Youth*): The organ of the Central Committee of the Communist Youth League. It began publication on April 27, 1951 in Beijing. Its main readership is composed of officials and members of the Youth League, and young people in general.

Zhongguo Shaonian Bao (*Chinese Children*): A paper for children, run by the Central Committee of the Communist Youth League. It began publication in September 1949 under the title *Zhongguo Ertong* (*Chinese Children*). In November 1951, it became a weekly and adopted its present name.

Tiyubao (*Sports*): Run by the State Physical Culture and Sports Commission. It publishes two issues a week. It was founded on September 10, 1956 in Beijing.

Shichang (*The Market*): Began publication on October 1, 1979. It is a weekly journal for producers and consumers, with reports on the economy and marketing news from home and abroad.

Newspapers are also published at the provincial, municipal and autonomous regional level. As well as reporting important national news, these newspapers concentrate on local news and developments. In addition there are evening papers in Kunming, Beijing, Nanchang, Guangzhou and other cities. These evening papers, which complement the dailies, are lively and informative tabloids.

The Chinese government has always paid great attention to the publication of newspapers for minority ethnic groups. In 1962, there were newspapers in 11 minority languages, namely Mongolian, Tibetan, Uygur, Kazak, Korean, Zhuang, Kirgiz, Dai, Jingpo, Lisu and Xibe. The total circulation of minority newspapers in 1978 was over 12,776 million copies.

(3) EDUCATION AND RESEARCH IN JOURNALISM

Education in journalism in China is just in the developmental stage. The Department of Journalism in the Graduate Studies Institute of the Chinese Academy of Social Sciences offers training in seven fields, namely journalistic theory, the history of Chinese journalism, the history of journalism in the Chinese Communist Party, world journalism, news writing, international reporting and news writing in English.

Newspapers in China, 1950-80*

Year	Number of Titles	Total Circulation (in ten thousand copies)
1950	382	79,752
1956	347	261,179
1957	364	244,244
1965	343	474,108
1966	49	367,198
1976	182	1,242,854
1979	69	1,308,242
1980	188	1,404,206
Total Circulation 1950-80		17,931,440

There are also departments of journalism in the Chinese People's University in Beijing, Fudan University in Shanghai, Ji'nan University in Guangzhou and the Beijing Broadcasting College. Courses in journalism are offered in Guangxi University, Wuhan University, Zhengzhou University, Xiamen (Amoy) University, Jiang-xi University and the Institute of International Politics. Students of journalism are given courses in literature, history and philosophy, as well as basic courses on ancient and modern Chinese language, Chinese history, logic and

* The circulation of newspapers at prefectural level in 1966, 1979 and 1980 is not included.

foreign languages. There are also courses on specialized professional subjects. For example, the Television Production Programme in Beijing Broadcasting College offers courses in music, art, photography, film editing, video and so on. The Journalism Programme in Ji'nan University has courses of foreign news and television designed for journalists stationed in Hong Kong, Macao and abroad.

Undergraduate courses are usually four years and postgraduate courses are three years.

The *People's Daily* runs a part-time college in journalism which provides in-service training for journalists. The Chinese Journalists' Association and the Chinese People's University have evening schools where journalists working in Beijing can be given training. The Institute of Journalism in the Chinese Academy of Social Sciences was founded in 1978, and was followed by research institutes in Heilongjiang, Jilin, Liaoning, Shaanxi and Shandong. Research institutions for journalism have also been set up by the Xinhua News Agency, *People's Daily* and some provincial papers.

2. RADIO AND TELEVISION

(1) A BRIEF HISTORY OF CHINESE BROADCASTING

In the spring of 1940, preparations were made for the founding of revolutionary broadcasting. On December 30, 1940, the Yan'an Xinhua Broadcasting Station, the first radio station to be set up by the Chinese revolutionaries, went on the air. The name was later changed to the Northern Shaanxi Xinhua Broadcasting Station. On March 25, 1949, it moved to Beijing. After the founding of the People's Republic it became known as the Central People's Broadcasting Station (CPBS) and began nation-wide transmission. Its overseas radio service began transmission in April 1950, under the call sign Radio Peking (Radio Beijing).

The progress of Chinese broadcasting in these 40 years has been rapid. A comprehensive broadcasting system reaches to every part of China, and includes foreign and domestic radio broadcasting, domestic television broadcasting and wired (diffusion) broadcast in the countryside.

Domestic broadcasting China's domestic broadcasting is divided into three levels: The Central People's Broadcasting Station; local radio stations run at the provincial, municipal and autonomous regional level, and wired broadcast stations in the countryside. At the end of 1980, there were 106 central and local broadcasting stations, 484 relay and transmitting stations, 102 frequency modulation stations and about 100 million radios. In the countryside, the main form of communication is wired broadcasting. The network is based on a system of commune broadcasting relay stations as the basic unit transmitting from county broadcasting stations at the centre. At the end of 1980, more than 2,500 counties (including banners) had broadcasting stations, over 49,000 people's communes (about 92 per cent of the total communes) had relay broadcasting stations, and there were 98.56 million loudspeakers in the countryside. This system enables more than 49 per cent of peasant families listen to broadcasts at home.

The CPBS broadcasts two comprehensive programmes to all parts of the country. It also broadcasts one programme to Taiwan Province, one to ethnic minority regions and one for overseas Chinese. It also has one frequency modulation programme. Programmes on local radio stations are geared to local needs.

Overseas broadcasting China's overseas radio service is provided by the Chinese International Broadcasting Station. Its call sign is Radio Peking (Radio Beijing). At the end of 1980, it broadcast in 38 foreign languages as well as in Chinese (*putonghua,* or "common speech", and four local dialects). Radio Beijing can now be heard in most parts of the world. Within Asia there are broadcasts in 24 languages: Arabic, Bengali, Burmese, Kampuchean, English, Turkish, Hindi, Indonesian, Japanese, Korean, Lao, Malay, Mongolian, Nepali, Tagalog, Pushtu, Russian, Sinhalese, Tamil, Thai, Urdu, Vietnamese, Esperanto and Persian.

African broadcasts are in 6 languages: Arabic, English, French, Hausa, Portuguese and Swahili.

Latin American broadcasts are in 3 languages: Spanish, Portuguese and Esperanto.

North American broadcasts are all in English.

European broadcasts are in 16 languages: Russian, German, Albanian, Romanian, Polish, Czech, Bulgarian, Serbo-Croatian, Hungarian, English, French, Italian, Spanish, Portuguese and Esperanto.

Oceanian broadcasts are all in English.

Broadcasts for overseas Chinese are in *putonghua* and Guangzhou (Cantonese), Xiamen, Kejia (Hakka) and Chaozhou (Chiuchow) dialects.

Television Chinese television broadcasting began in 1958; colour transmission began in May 1973 using the West German PAL system. Now all provinces, centrally administered municipalities and autonomous regions have their own TV stations. At the end of 1980, there were 38 TV stations, and 246 transmitting and relay stations, each with a capacity of more than 1,000 watts, in China. There were also more than 1,000 translator stations (small capacity relay stations which can receive programmes from one channel and switch them to another channel). With the exception of Tibet, Inner Mongolia and Xinjiang, all parts of the country can relay Chinese Central Television (CCTV) programmes in addition to preparing their own programmes. TV can now be seen in more than 30 per cent of districts throughout China. At the end of 1980, there were more than 8 million TV receivers in China. In 1972, a ground satellite station was set up in Beijing, which assists in domestic and international programme exchanges.

Chinese broadcasting administration The Central Broadcasting Administrative Bureau under the State Council is responsible for control of broadcasting, television, recording and so on. The provinces, prefectures and counties also have broadcasting administrative bureaus for the administration of local radio stations, television stations and wired-broadcasting networks. The state radio stations, TV stations and technological departments under the Central Broadcasting Administrative Bureau have professional contacts with more than 70 countries and regions, contacts with 9 international bodies, and broadcast and television co-operative agreements with 12 countries.

The China Record Company, the Chinese Broadcasting Troupe, the Broadcasting Research Institute and the Beijing Broadcasting College are also administered by the Central Broadcasting Administrative Bureau. The China Record Company is responsible for selecting, editing, recording and processing master tapes of programmes on music, opera and cultural and educational broadcasts,

which are handed over to the recording industry for
making records and cassette tapes. It also handles the
export of records and recorded programmes. It issues
long-playing and plastic film records and cassette tapes
(mono and stereo). In 1980, it produced 5,669,700 long-
playing records and 55,794,500 plastic film records. There
is one record factory in Shanghai, one in Beijing and one
in Chengdu.

The Chinese Broadcasting Troupe was set up in 1951
for direct use by radio and television stations. It has 5
divisions, an orchestra, a traditional orchestra, a chorus,
a TV drama troupe and a popular entertainment troupe.
The Chinese Broadcasting Traditional Orchestra has
performed in more than ten countries and regions in
Europe, Oceania and Asia in recent years. The Broadcasting Research Institute is responsible for scientific and
technological research on radio and television broadcasting. The Ministry of Posts and Telecommunications
supplies microwave lines for long-distance programmes,
and the Central Broadcasting Administrative Bureau and
local broadcasting administrative bureaus are responsible
for all other technical aspects of broadcasting.

The Beijing Broadcasting College, the only college
specializing in training broadcasting personnel, was set
up by the Central Broadcasting Administrative Bureau in
1959. Its students learn journalism, foreign languages,
literature and art, and broadcasting technology, and about
3,000 have graduated since 1959.

(2) BROADCASTING AND TELEVISION STATIONS

The Central People's Broadcasting Station The Central
People's Broadcasting Station (CPBS) is the state radio

station of the People's Republic of China. Its programme coverage includes general and specific policies of the state and the Communist Party, domestic and world news, cultural and scientific knowledge, and light entertainment. The CPBS broadcasts daily on six separate channels for a total of more than 95 hours. Two channels broadcast in *putonghua* for 40 hours and 30 minutes per day. The third, beamed to Taiwan Province, broadcasts in *putonghua* and in the southern Fujian and Kejia (Hakka) dialects for 20 hours and 50 minutes per day. The fourth, beamed to ethnic minority regions, broadcasts in Mongolian, Tibetan, Uygur, Kazak and Korean for 12 hours per day. The fifth broadcasts for overseas Chinese in *putonghua*, and the Guangzhou (Cantonese), Kejia (Hakka), Xiamen, and Chaozhou (Chiuchow) dialects for 16 hours per day. In May 1980, the CPBS set up a mono frequency modulation broadcast which concentrates on music and opera broadcasting for 5 hours and 30 minutes per day. Comprehensive programmes are offered in 144 channels by radio stations run by provinces, centrally administered municipalities and autonomous regions.

The programmes may be divided into three categories. The first is news, which accounts for 15 per cent of total programming. The second is specialized programming, which accounts for 20 per cent of total programming. Specialized programming includes programmes for specialized audiences, such as peasants, preschool children, youth, children, and PLA soldiers, a Listeners' Letter Box, programmes for Taiwan Province and so on; programmes on special subjects include Theoretical Studies, Scientific Knowledge, Sports, Scientific Agriculture, Hygiene, Reading and Appreciation, Across China, Around the

World and English by Radio. The third is light entertainment, which accounts for 60 per cent of total programming and includes music, opera, story-telling, comic dia-
logues, radio plays, film sound-tracks, drama and listeners' choice programmes. There are also programme an-
nouncements, physical exercises to music, advertisement
and so on, which account for 5 per cent of total programming.

The Chinese International Broadcasting Station The
Chinese International Broadcasting Station makes radio
broadcasts to all parts of the world. Its original name was
Radio Peking. It was set up in April 1950, braodcasting
in English, Japanese, Korean, Vietnamese, Thai, Burmese
and Indonesian. Its present name was adopted in May
1978, but its call sign is still Radio Peking (Radio Beijing). It now broadcasts in 38 foreign languages,
putonghua and four local dialects for a total of 136 hours
per day. In 1980 it received 90,000 letters from foreign
listeners in 136 countries and regions throughout the
world and from Chinese in Hong Kong and Macao. Programmes include news, commentaries, music and special
programmes such as China Reconstructs, Reports from the
Countryside, Chinese Culture, Society and Life, Travel in
China, Learning Chinese and Listeners' Letter Box. It
has a programme exchange with radio stations in more
than 20 countries, and its own correspondents in Japan,
France, Yugoslavia and so on.

Chinese Central Television Chinese Central Television
(CCTV) is the state television station of the People's Republic of China, broadcasting on channels two and eight.
Its original name was Peking Television. Experimental
broadcasting began on May 1, 1958, and the station was
formally inaugurated on September 2 the same year. Its

present name was adopted on May 1, 1978. CCTV began transmitting in colour in May 1973, using the West German PAL system. CCTV now has two programmes in full colour, one national and one local (Beijing). The national programming includes both general and educational programmes (lectures and the open university). The local Beijing channel provides general programming, offering Beijing residents a choice. The two channels broadcast for a total of 100 hours per week, 76 hours on the national channel, 23 hours and 19 minutes on the local channel. All provinces, centrally administered municipalities and autonomous regions have their own programmes and relay the CCTV national programmes. The CCTV national programme consists of news (13.5 per cent), sports (4.5 per cent), light entertainment (52 per cent) and special items (30 per cent). CCTV began transmitting international news via satellite on April 1, 1980. It now has a telefilm exchange with TV organizations in more than 30 countries and regions.

(1)   The Development of Broadcasting in China

Year	TV stations	Radio stations	Wired broadcast stations	Wired broadcast loudspeakers (in ten thousand)
1949		49	11	0.09
1957		61	1,698	94.1
1965	12	87	2,365	872.5
1978	32	93	2,555	11,211.9
1979	38	99	2,560	10,771.6
1980	38	106	2,610	9,856.6

(2) Timetable of Broadcasting to
the World in Commonly Used Languages

Language	Beijing time	GMT (Greenwich Mean Time)	Region	Wave band (metre)
English	08:00–09:00	00:00–01:00	Eastern North America	19,16
	09:00–10:00	01:00–02:00		19,16
	10:00–11:00	02:00–03:00		
	20:00–21:00	12:00–13:00		25,19
	11:00–12:00	03:00–04:00	Western North America	19,16
	12:00–13:00	04:00–05:00		
	16:30–17:30	08:30–09:30	South Pacific	30,25,19,16
	17:30–18:30	09:30–10:30		
	20:00–21:00	12:00–13:00	Southeast Asia	25,19,16
	21:00–22:00	13:00–14:00		
	22:00–23:00	14:00–15:00	South Asia	25,19,16
	23:00–24:00	15:00–16:00		
	00:00–02:00	16:00–18:00	East and South Africa	25,19,16
	03:30–05:30	19:30–21:30	West and North Africa	31,26,19

Language	Beijing time	GMT (Greenwich Mean Time)	Region	Wave band (metre)
English	04:30–05:30	20:30–21:30	Europe	30,26
	05:30–06:30	21:30–22:30		
French	02:30–03:30	18:30–19:30	Africa	42,24,38,19
	04:30–05:30	20:30–21:30		
	03:30–04:30	19:30–20:30	Europe	42,24,38,19
	05:30–06:30	21:30–22:30		
Russian	00:00–01:00	16:00–17:00	Europe and Asia	25,31,40,42, 49,58,196
	01:00–02:00	17:00–18:00		25,31,40,42, 45,58,196
	02:00–03:00	18:00–19:00		25,31,40,42, 196
	03:00–04:00	19:00–20:00		25,31,40,42, 196
	04:00–05:00	20:00–21:00		31,42,196
	05:00–06:00	21:00–22:00		196
	06:00–07:00	22:00–23:00		196
	11:00–12:00	3:00–4:00		19,25
	18:00–19:00	10:00–11:00		16,19,25,31, 42,45
	19:00–20:00	11:00–12:00		25,31,45,49

Language	Beijing time	GMT (Greenwich Mean Time)	Region	Wave band (metre)
Russian	21:00–22:00	13:00–14:00	Europe and Asia	25,31,42, 196,228
	23:00–24:00	15:00–16:00		25,31,38,40, 42,58,196
Spanish	07:00–08:00	23:00–24:00	Latin America	26,19,16
	08:00–09:00	00:00–01:00		26,19,16
	09:00–10:00	01:00–02:00		25,19,16
	10:00–11:00	02:00–03:00		25,19,16
	19:00–19:30	11:00–11:30		19,16
	19:30–20:00	11:30–12:00		19,16
	05:00–07:00	21:00–23:00	Europe	40,31,25
Arabic	00:30–01:30	16:30–17:30	North Africa and West Asia	40,31,26
	02:30–03:30	18:30–19:30		
	05:30–06:30	21:30–22:30		
Japanese	06:30–07:00	22:30–23:00	Japan	288,40,25
	18:30–23:30	10:30–15:30		
Chinese (putonghua)	01:30–02:30	17:30–18:30	Western Europe, North Africa and Europe	47,45,31,30, 25,24
	04:00–05:00	20:00–21:00		31,26,42,40

Language	Beijing time	GMT (Greenwich Mean Time)	Region	Wave band (metre)
Chinese (*putonghua*)	06:30-07:00	22:30-23:00	Southeast Asia	51,47,42,30, 25
	10:00-11:00	02:00-03:00	Eastern North America, Central and South America	25,19,16
	12:00-13:00	04:00-05:00	Western North America	19,16
	17:00-18:00	09:00-10:00	South Pacific and Southeast Asia	31,24,19
	21:00-22:00	13:00-14:00	Southeast Asia	31,24,19
	23:00-24:00	15:00-16:00	South Asia and Southeast Asia	31,19

3. BOOKS AND PERIODICALS

(1) PERIODICALS

Early Chinese periodicals The earliest periodical published in China in Chinese was *A Study of the East and West*, a monthly founded in Guangzhou in 1833 by foreign missionaries. It became the Western colonialists' weapon for economic and cultural aggression against China. The earliest periodical run by Chinese was the *Aomen Yuebao* (*Macao Monthly*) founded in 1839 by the Qing official Lin Zexu, as part of his campaign to ban opium.

Pre-Liberation progressive periodicals Shortly before the May 4 Movement of 1919, progressive intellectuals began the struggle to oppose feudalism and spread democratic ideas. The monthly *Xin Qingnian* (*New Youth*) initiated and was the main battleground for the struggle.

In 1915, Chen Duxiu, who became one of the first leaders of the Chinese Communist Party, published in Shanghai a magazine by the name of *Qingnian Zazhi* (*Youth*). For the second volume, the name was changed to *Xin Qingnian* (*New Youth*), and in 1916 it moved to Beijing. Li Dazhao, one of the founders of the Chinese Communist Party, and Lu Xun, the famous writer, were among those who took part in the editorial work at various stages. The magazine formed a meeting ground for progressive intellectuals and gradually became the centre of the new cultural movement. After the victory of the Russian October Revolution in 1917, Li Dazhao published two articles in the *New Youth* ("A Comparison Between the French Revolution and the Russian Revolution" and "The Victory of Bolshevism"), in which he hailed the October Revolution and called on the Chinese people to welcome the new revolutionary trend. The *New Youth* became a fervent advocate of Marxism. The May 4 Movement of 1919 brought an enormous increase to the number of periodicals in circulation. Among the most famous were the *Xiangjiang Pinglun* (*The Xiangjiang River Review*) founded by Mao Zedong; the weekly *Laodongjie* (*Labour Circles*) and the monthly *Gongchandang* (*Communist*

Party), both founded by the Shanghai Party Group; the weekly *Laodong Yin* (*Voice of Labour*) founded by the Beijing Party Group, and the weekly *Laodongzhe* (*The Worker*) founded by the Guangzhou Party Group. These magazines played a great role in propagating the integration of Marxism-Leninism with the labour movement and promoting China's new democratic revolution.

After its founding, the Chinese Communist Party set up the *Xiangdao Zhoukan* (*Guide Weekly*), its first central organ, published in Shanghai from September 1922 to July 1927; the *Qianfeng* (*Vanguard*), a quarterly published in Guangzhou from July 1923 to February 1924; and the quarterly *Xin Qingnian* (*New Youth*), published in Guangzhou from June 1923 to July 1926. The weekly *Zhongguo Qingnian* (*Chinese Youth*) published in Shanghai from October 1923 to October 1927 was the organ of the Communist Youth League Central Committee; under the slogan "to the masses", it encouraged young people to devote themselves to the workers' and peasants' revolutionary movement, and was one of the most influential magazines of its time. Later periodicals include the *Buersheweike* (*Bolshevik*), published in Shanghai from October 1927 to July 1932; *Hongqi* (*Red Flag*), founded in Shanghai in 1931; the weekly *Jiefang (Liberation)*, April 1937 to the autumn of 1941, founded in Yan'an as the political and theoretical organ of the Central Committee of the Communist Party of China; and the weekly *Qunzhong* (*The Masses*), founded in Hankou in December 1937 as the aboveground journal of the Communist Party in the Kuomintang areas.

In the 1920s there were also periodicals published by revolutionary literary societies set up by progressive intellectuals, such as the Literary Research Society, the

Creation Society, the Thread of Talk Society and the Unnamed Society. The magazines published by the League of Left-Wing Writers in the 1930s were also very influential.

Periodicals in New China Since Liberation, the number of periodicals in China has greatly increased. In 1965, there were 790 national, provincial and local periodicals, more than 2.5 times the figure for 1950. During the "cultural revolution", most periodicals were forced to cease publication. For example, the 14 periodicals published by the Department of Philosophy and Social Sciences of the Chinese Academy of Sciences were all forced to cease publication. In 1971 there were only 77 national, provincial and local periodicals, only one-tenth of the 1965 figure.

After 1976, periodicals began to flourish again: 930 periodicals were published in 1978. In 1979, 1,470 periodicals (75 per cent being scientific and technological periodicals) were published, a 71 per cent increase over the figure for 1964 (856). In 1980, 2,191 periodicals were published, an increase of 156 per cent over 1964. Of the 1980 figure, 1,384, or 63 per cent, were scientific or technological publications, 265 were on literature and art, 210 were on the social sciences and 332 on other subjects. At present the main national periodicals are as follows:

Hongqi (*Red Flag*), the theoretical organ of the Central Committee; a monthly founded on June 1, 1958.

Zhongguo Qingnian (*Chinese Youth*), organ of the Central Committee of the Communist Youth League; a monthly, founded in October 1923 in Shanghai.

Zhongguo Funü (*Women of China*), organ of the All-China Women's Federation; a monthly, founded in 1949. Originally called *Xin Zhongguo Funü* (*Women of New*

China), it adopted its present name in 1956. It is published in Chinese and English.

Zhongguo Ertong (*Children of China*), a monthly founded by the Communist Youth League Central Committee for junior primary school students; began publication in 1980.

Zhexue Yanjiu (*Philosophical Research*), a monthly sponsored by the Institute of Philosophy of the Chinese Academy of Social Sciences; began publication in 1955.

Lishi Yanjiu (*Historical Research*), a monthly sponsored by the Chinese Academy of Social Sciences; began publication in 1954.

Faxue Yanjiu (*Legal Research*), a bi-monthly sponsored by the Institute of Law of the Chinese Academy of Social Sciences; began publication in April 1979.

Zhongguo Shehui Kexue (*Social Sciences in China*), a publication of the Chinese Academy of Social Sciences; began publication on January 10, 1980. A comprehensive academic journal mainly for presenting recent achievements in scientific research in philosophy and social sciences in China. It is published as a bi-monthly in Chinese and as a quarterly in English.

Jingji Yanjiu (*Economic Research*), a monthly sponsored by the Institute of Economics; began publication in 1955.

Renmin Jiaoyu (*People's Education*), a monthly sponsored by the Ministry of Education; began publication in 1950.

Kaogu (*Archaeology*), a bi-monthly sponsored by the Institute of Archaeology of the Chinese Academy of Social Sciences; began publication in 1955. Originally called *Kaogu Tongxun* (*Archaeological Reports*), it adopted its present name in 1959.

Wenwu (*Cultural Relics*), a monthly sponsored by the

Bureau of Museums and Archaeological Materials; began publication in 1950. Originally known as *Wenwu Cankao (Reference Materials on Cultural Relics)*, it adopted its present name in 1959.

Dili Zhishi (Geography), a monthly jointly sponsored by the Chinese Geographical Society and the Institute of Geography of the Chinese Academy of Sciences; began publication in 1950.

Wenyi Bao (Literary Gazette), a monthly review of literature sponsored by the Union of Chinese Writers; began publication in September 1949.

Renmin Wenxue (People's Literature), a monthly, the organ of the Union of Chinese Writers; began publication in October 1949.

Shijie Wenxue (World Literature), successor to *Yiwen (Translations)*, founded by Lu Xun in 1933 and republished in Beijing in 1953; adopted its present name in 1959. It is sponsored by the Institute of Foreign Literature of the Chinese Academy of Social Sciences.

Wenxue Pinglun (Literary Review), a bi-monthly, began publication in 1957. Originally called *Wenxue Yanjiu (Literary Research)*, it adopted its present name in January 1959.

Renmin Xiju (People's Drama), a monthly review sponsored by the Chinese Dramatists' Association; began publication in April 1950. It features theoretical articles along with articles of general interest.

Renmin Yinyue (People's Music), a monthly sponsored by the Chinese Musicians' Association; began publication in 1950.

Dazhong Dianying (Popular Cinema), a monthly sponsored by the Chinese Film Artists' Association; began publication in 1950.

Dianying Yishu (*Film Arts*), a monthly sponsored by the Chinese Film Artists' Association. The result of a merger in July 1959 of *Zhongguo Dianying* (*Chinese Cinema*), which began publication in 1956, and *Guoji Dianying* (*International Cinema*), which began publication in 1958.

Jiefangjun Huabao (*Liberation Army Pictorial*), a fortnightly edited and published by the General Political Department of the Chinese People's Liberation Army; began publication in 1951.

Minzu Huabao (*Ethnic Pictorial*), a monthly published by the Minorities Press; began publication in 1955.

Meishu (*Fine Arts*), sponsored by the Chinese National Artists' Association; began publication in February 1950.

(1) Periodicals in 1980

Subject	Number
General	58
Social Sciences	210
Natural Sciences and Technology	1,384
Culture and Education	179
Literature and Art	265
Juvenile	43
Pictorial	52
Total	2,191

(2) Periodicals in 1950-80

Year	Number	Circulation (in ten thousand copies)
1950	295	3,530
1956	484	35,265
1957	634	31,500
1965	790	44,066
1966	191	23,441
1969	20	4,589
1976	542	55,783
1979	1,470	118,373
1980	2,191	112,479
Total Circulation 1950-80		1,093,869

(2) BOOKS

Brief History of Book Publication in China China's pictographic writing was already in a fairly advanced state by the 14th century B.C. At first the characters were inscribed on tortoise-shells and ox bones; afterwards, they were inscribed on bronzes or written on bamboo or wooden slips or fabrics of various kinds. These means enabled greater circulation and were the precursors of

books. Book publication proper began with the invention
of papermaking and printing. Around the 10th century,
Chinese book publication extended from great quantities
of individual works into large-scale collections, reference
works and encyclopaedias. Some consisted of many
fascicles and covered a wide range of subjects. Examples
are the four major works compiled at the end of the 10th
century: *Wenyuan Yinghua* (*Choice Blossoms from the
Garden of Literature*), *Taiping Yulan* (*Taiping Imperial
Readings*), *Cefu Yuangui* (*Encyclopaedia of History*) and
Taiping Guangji (*Taiping Collectanea*); the first three in
about 1,000 fascicles and the last in 500 fascicles. The
Yongle Dadian (*Yongle Encyclopaedia*), compiled in the
15th century, was in more than 22,900 fascicles and more
than 370,000,000 characters. The *Siku Quanshu* (*Complete
Library of the Four Treasuries of Knowledge*), compiled
in the 1770s, was in more than 79,000 fascicles. Early in
the 18th century, the *Gujin Tushu Jicheng* (*Collection of
Books, Ancient and Modern*) was printed from copper
movable type and published in 10,000 fascicles and about
100,000,000 characters. According to catalogues from the
past that it is possible to examine, in the more than 2,000
years between the Western Han and the Qing dynasties,
approximately 181,000 books in altogether 2,360,000
fascicles were published.

After the mid-19th century, China began to use
modern printing technology, including letterpress and
lithography. Modern presses and periodical publishers
were established, such as the Commercial Press, founded
in 1897, and the China Publishing House, founded in 1912.
These fairly large and modern publishers brought out
books introducing Western bourgeois democratic ideas,
science and technology, and in this way helped to pro-

mote the early democratic revolution and cultural enlightenment movement.

Progressive book publication in China started with the
May 4 Movement of 1919. The Cultural Press in Hunan
and the People's Press in Guangzhou, both founded by
the Chinese Communist Party, became powerful instruments in propagating revolutionary ideas in the 1920s. In
1939 the Xinhua (New China) Bookstore was founded in
Yan'an, the seat of the Central Committee of the Chinese
Communist Party, to handle printing, publication and
distribution as a single unit. Xinhua bookstores were also
set up in other liberated areas. On the eve of Liberation
in 1949, there were more than 700 Xinhua bookstores
throughout the country. Operating under extremely difficult conditions in a tense wartime environment, they
nevertheless published a large number of books and
periodicals. Between 1940 and August 1949, a total of
44,740,000 copies of 5,300 books were published in the
liberated areas. The Xinhua bookstores played an extremely important role in spreading Marxism-Leninism,
publicizing the Party's policies and supporting culture
and education. During the 1930s, the Life Books, New
Knowledge Books and the Study Press (amalgamated in
1948 as the Sanlian Shudian, or Joint Publishing Company) operated in the Kuomintang areas, forming the main
core of revolutionary and progressive publishing at that
time. Under the leadership of the Chinese Communist
Party, the Joint Publishing Company printed, published
and distributed a large number of books and periodicals,
making an important contribution to the spread of revolutionary ideas and culture.

Publishing in New China After the founding of the
People's Republic, the Chinese government adopted a

series of important measures for developing book publishing. First the Xinhua bookstores formerly under decentralized management were merged to form a national state publishing enterprise, and state publishing developed steadily. The publishing sections were then detached from the original Xinhua bookstores and became independent enterprises, operating as the Central People's Press and People's Press on the provincial, municipal and autonomous regional level. Next, according to law, publishing enterprises run by the reactionary government or by the bureaucrat-capitalist class were confiscated, and all decrees restricting freedom in publishing enacted by the reactionary government were abrogated. Thirdly, private capitalist publishing enterprises were re-organized and reformed, becoming joint state-private enterprises. From 1949 to 1956, book publishing developed quickly. Large numbers of socialist state publishing organizations and joint state-private enterprises were set up, and the variety and quantity of books printed increased by a large margin. The quality also gradually improved. In 1956, a total of 1,784.37 million copies of 28,773 books were published throughout the country, 127 per cent and 110 per cent respectively above the 1952 figure. There were 9,375 books on literature and art, 3,727 on philosophy and the social sciences, 8,698 on natural science and technology, 2,391 on culture and education and 8,997 juvenile books. Between 1949 and 1956, 241 works by Marx, Engels, Lenin and Stalin were published, along with the first three volumes of the *Selected Works of Mao Zedong* and the first three volumes of the *Complete Works of Lu Xun* (annotated). Over 4,900 books in Mongolian, Tibetan, Uygur, Kazak, Korean and Xibe were published, and over 15,700 foreign works from 43 countries were translated and published.

Between 1957 and 1965, a large number of good quality publications continued to appear. In 1959, the publication of the *Collected Works of Lenin* (39 volumes) and the *Collected Works of Marx and Engels* (19 volumes) was completed and in 1960, a newly edited *Selected Works of Lenin* (4 volumes) appeared. In 1965, publications of a new edition of the *Selected Works of Marx and Engels* in 4 volumes got under way, and in the same year Volume 4 of the *Selected Works of Mao Zedong* and Editions A and B of *Selected Readings from the Works of Mao Zedong* were published. In 1958, publication of the 10-volume *Complete Works of Lu Xun* and *Collected Translations by Lu Xun* was completed. Novels published in this period include *The Song of Youth*, *Red Crag*, *Red Sun*, *Keep the Red Flag Flying*, *Builders of a New Life*, *Great Changes in a Mountain Village*, *Steeled and Tempered* and *Tracks in the Snowy Forest*; revolutionary reminiscences also appeared, such as *A Single Spark Can Start a Prairie Fire*. About 100 books in the humanities for college and university use were published, including academic works of considerable value.

Like everything else, publishing suffered serious damage during the "cultural revolution". Many publishers were closed down and their staff dismissed. Large numbers of books were regarded as "poisonous weeds", vestiges of feudalism, capitalism and revisionism. Academic works, books on science and technology and reference books almost ceased publication entirely, creating a serious book shortage. During the decade of the "cultural revolution", an average of 7,903 titles were published annually, only 27.5 per cent of the 1956 figure.

After 1976, publishing took a turn for the better. The publishers that had closed down gradually resumed business and several dozen new publishers were set up. In 1980, a total of 4,592.98 million copies of 21,621 books and pictorial albums were published, of which 1,900 million copies of 15,669 titles were books. The increase in varieties and number of copies printed relieved the shortage, and publishing is developing steadily forward.

Reference books   In the 50 years preceding Liberation, about 260 Chinese and foreign-language dictionaries on language and literature and more than 70 dictionaries of science and technology were published in China. The best-known dictionaries include the *Ciyuan* (*Origins of Words and Phrases*), *Cihai* (*Dictionary of Words and Phrases*), *Citong* (*Analysis of Words and Phrases*), and *Zhonghua Dazidian* (*Comprehensive Chinese Dictionary*). From 1949 to 1965, 540 dictionaries of various kinds in a total of 77,000,000 copies appeared in China. Between 1977 and 1979, there were 80 new general dictionaries in Chinese and foreign languages and 140 topical dictionaries, in more than 55 million copies. A new three-volume edition of the *Cihai* was published in October 1979, and afterwards reprinted in a reduced format. This is the first revision of a major comprehensive dictionary since the founding of the People's Republic. The new *Cihai* has over 106,000 entries in 13,400,000 characters and with 3,000 illustrations. Two volumes of a four-volume *Ciyuan*, a medium-sized reference work on classical Chinese, have also been published. The complete work will have over 100,000 entries in about 10 million characters. China's first major encyclopaedia will be published in a series of volumes arranged by subject. The volume on astronomy was published in 1980. The complete work will cover more than 70 subjects and will take about 10 years to publish. A series of yearbooks has appeared, such as the *1980 Encyclopaedic Yearbook of China, 1980 Yearbook of Chinese Publications, 1980 Yearbook of Chinese History* and *1980 Yearbook of the World Economy.* The publication of the *Chinese Medical Encyclopaedia,* in 88 volumes with 35 million characters, began in 1980 and will appear volume by volume.

In addition to *Cihai* and *Ciyuan,* other language and literature dictionaries include *A Dictionary of Modern Chinese, A New Dictionary on the Four Corner System* (revised edition 1979), *A Short Chinese Dictionary, Dictionary of Words in Common Use in Ancient Chinese* and *A Dictionary of Chinese Idioms.* Specialized dictionaries include *A Concise Dictionary of Traditional Chinese Medicine, A Traditional Chinese Pharmacopoeia, A Dictionary of Agriculture, A Concise Dictionary of Animal Husbandry, A Concise Dictionary of Veterinary Science, An English-Chinese Technical Dictionary* and *A Concise English-Chinese Dictionary of Science and Technology.* New bilingual dictionaries include *A Chinese-English Dictionary, An English-Chinese Dictionary of New Terms, A Short English-Chinese Dictionary, A New Japanese-Chinese Dictionary, A Chinese-Russian Dictionary, A Russian-Chinese Dictionary of New Terms, A Concise German-Chinese Dictionary* and *A French-Chinese Dictionary.* New dictionaries for minority languages include *A Mongolian-Han Dictionary, A Mongolian Phonetic and Orthographic Dictionary, A Concise Dictionary of Mongolian Idioms, A New Tibetan*

Dictionary, A Han-Uygur Dictionary, A Short Uygur-Han Dictionary and *A Han-Kazak Dictionary.*

Books on philosophy and the social sciences Between 1950 and 1980, a total of 13,351.42 million copies of 64,192 books (including 54,734 new titles) on philosophy and the social sciences were published in China. Marxist-Leninist works and works by Mao Zedong occupied the first place in this category.

Publication of the *Collected Works of Stalin* in Chinese began in 1953 and was completed in 1956 in 13 volumes. Publication of the *Collected Works of Lenin* in Chinese began in 1955 and was completed in 1959 in 39 volumes. Publication of the *Collected Works of Marx and Engels* began at the end of 1956, and over 40 volumes have appeared in Chinese. Selections from the Marxist-Leninist classics include the *Selected Works of Marx and Engels* in four volumes, *Selected Works of Lenin* in four volumes and *Selected Works of Mao Zedong* in five volumes.

In addition to the classics themselves there are also theoretical works by various scholars. Recent examples of considerable academic standing include *Theoretical Problems of a Socialist Economy* and *China's Socialist Economy* by Xue Muqiao, *Theoretical Problems of a Socialist Economy* by Sun Yefang, *Regulation and Planning in a Commodity Economy* by Deng Liqun, *The Economic Results of Socialist Production* by Yu Guangyuan, *Socialist Production, Circulation and Distribution* by Xu Dixin, *The History of Western Aesthetics* by Zhu Guangqian, *A Perspective on Literature* by Qian Zhongshu, *An Outline of Materialist Dialectics* by Li Da, *A Critique of Critiques* (*A Review of Kant's Philosophy*) by Li Zehou and *An Outline History of Christianity* by Yang Zhen. China's heritage of ancient books has also received a great amount of scholarly attention. The 24 dynastic histories, a series of valuable historical records in 3,249 fascicles in 40 million characters, are difficult to read and use because of their lack of punctuation and many errors in transcription. For the first time in Chinese publishing history, the huge project of correcting and punctuating them in modern style has now been undertaken and publication has been completed within 20 years. The *Complete Bone and Tortoise Shell Inscriptions*, edited by the late Guo Moruo in 13 volumes, has also appeared, an important event in the history of archaic orthography. *A Historical Atlas of China* is a very recent publication which took many years to prepare.

Books on science and technology Between 1950 and 1980, a total of 2,797.61 million copies of 121,607 books (including 86,082 new titles) on science and technology were published in China. The National Conference on Science and Technology in 1978 gave a considerable boost to scientific and technological publishing. In 1980, 5,715 books on science and technology were published, 138 per cent above the 1976 figure of 2,400. Recent publications include the *Collected Works of Zhu Kezhen, An Introduction to Geomechanics* and *Methods of Geomechanics* by Li Siguang, *An Introduction to the Theory of Mathematics* by Hua Luogeng, *A Calculus of Variations and Finite Elements* by Qian Weichang, *Elementary Theory in Mathematics* by Chen Jingrun, *Fixed Point Class Theory* by Jiang Zehan and *Methods in Ligand Field Theory* by Tang Aoqing. A translation of Einstein's *Collected Works* has also been published. Science and technology presses have been set up in 12 provinces and centrally administered municipalities publishing and distributing large numbers of books, periodicals, dictionaries and handbooks. These materials play an active role in scientific research, teaching and production.

Literary works Between 1950 and 1980, a total of 4,844.65 million copies of 110,609 books (including 78,467 new titles) in the field of literature were published in China. In 1980, about 100 novels were published, more than in any previous year. Many excellent older works have also been reprinted in recent years, such as *Red Crag, The Song of Youth* and *The Second Blooming* (a collection of short stories). Lu Xun's works have been published in many different forms, including a complete collection, selections, single editions and photostat reproductions of original manuscripts. On September 25, 1981, on the eve of the centenary of Lu Xun's birthday, a new edition of the *Complete Works of Lu Xun* in 16 volumes with annotation came out. It adds six volumes (about 2 million characters) of previously unknown works, prefaces to his translations and editions of ancient books, letters and diaries to the 10-volume 1958 edition. The complete works of the famous writer Guo Moruo are being edited for publication, and works by old writers such as Mao Dun, Ba Jin, Lao She, Cao Yu, Zhou Libo and some newer writers are also being published. The translation and publication of famous works of foreign literature has been steadily increasing, with the publication of Shakespeare's *Complete Works, Conversations with Goethe, My Past and Thoughts* by Herzen and so on.

Children's books More than 3,400 new books for young people have been published by the Chinese Youth Press and the Chinese Children's Press since Liberation, with a total circulation of 580 million copies. Books on political education amount to one-third of the whole. Series on popular science have been well received by young readers, such as *Natural Sciences for Children* and *One Hundred Thousand Whys*. Excellent literary works have a large circulation; for instance, more than 6 million copies of *Red Crag* have been printed. Science fiction has also been popular with young readers in recent years.

The Chinese government is greatly concerned with children's education. About 1,000 writers now specialize in children's literature and research societies on children's literature have been set up in many places.

Books in minority languages China is a multi-ethnic country, and the translation and publication of minority language material has an important place in Chinese publishing. The Minorities Press was founded in 1953 in Beijing as a national organization for publishing books and periodicals in minority languages. The Minority Languages Translation and Publishing Bureau was founded in 1974 in Beijing to translate and publish works by Marx, Engels, Lenin, Stalin and Mao Zedong, along with other political, economic and literary works, in Mongolian, Tibetan, Uygur, Kazak, Korean and so on. Some provinces and autonomous regions also publish books and periodicals in local minority languages. There are at present 15 presses which concentrate books in minority languages in China. According to incomplete figures, a total of 34.27 million copies of 1,921 books (including 1,456 new titles) were published in minority languages in 1980. The number of titles is 24.4 per cent above the 1979 figure and the circulation is 26.6 per cent above that in 1979. Political books have an important place in minority language publishing. Mao Zedong's *Selected Works* and Marxist-Leninist works have been published in Mongolian, Tibetan, Uygur, Kazak and Korean. The famous Chinese classics such as *A Dream of*

Red Mansions, Romance of the Three Kingdoms and *Outlaws of the Marsh* and important works by Lu Xun, Guo Moruo and Mao Dun have also been translated into minority languages. The publication of dictionaries is of even greater importance. Of China's 55 ethnic minorities, only the Hui, Manchu and She use the Han Chinese language; the others have their own languages. Since the founding of the People's Republic, 41 dictionaries in minority languages have been published.

Books in braille Publishing in braille has had a gradual development in New China. The Chinese Welfare Association for the Blind has a publishing centre which issued 17,000 copies of 44 books in braille in 1954. Mao Zedong's *Selected Works* in four volumes were published in braille between 1964 and 1966. The Beijing Braille Press was founded in 1978 under the direct guidance of the State Administration of Publications. About 200 books in braille were published in 1980, and 5 periodicals: *Knowledge and Life, Scientific Knowledge, Young Science, Hygiene* and *Literary Selections.*

To sum up, publishing in China has developed rapidly after some reorganization and recovery in recent years. This development is illustrated in the following tables.

(3) PUBLISHING ORGANIZATIONS

State Administration of Publications This is an administrative unit under the State Council for directing and managing national publishing. Its main task is to supervise the implementation of state general and specific policies in publishing, to coordinate relations between publishing, printing and distribution, to unify arrange-

(1) Book Publication

Year	Number of titles	Number of copies (in ten thousand copies)
1971	7,771	242,108
1977	12,886	330,804
1980	21,621	459,298

(2) Types of Publications

Year	Philosophy and social sciences	Literature and art	Science and technology	Culture and education
1971	1,847	404	911	121
1977	2,057	1,253	2,857	455
1980	2,091	3,322	5,715	2,095

ments for distributing paper and printing materials for newspaper and book publication, to coordinate publishing units in organizing writers and translators, and to promote the publication of books of all kinds.

The Association of Chinese Publishers This is a mass organization of a specialized nature voluntarily formed by Chinese publishers. It was founded on December 20, 1979 in Changsha, with Hu Yuzhi as Honorary Chairman and Chen Hanbo as Chairman. The purpose of this organization is to develop and promote publishing in China.

Publishing houses There are 192 publishing houses and 15,000 people working in the publishing profession in China today. Publishing is concentrated in Beijing and Shanghai which account for 60 per cent of all publishing in China, with 94 presses in Beijing and 14 in Shanghai. Beijing is the national publishing centre. Most of the presses in Beijing and Shanghai specialize in particular fields, and only a few are of a general nature. The presses at the provincial level are of both kinds. On the average, there are two presses in each province, centrally administered municipality or autonomous region, but a few have three or four presses.

A Brief Introduction to the Major Presses in China

A. Presses Under the State Administration of Publications:

Renmin Chubanshe (People's Press) was founded in December 1950 mainly to publish the works of Marx, Engels, Lenin, Stalin and Mao Zedong, Party and government documents, books on the social sciences (such as philosophy, economics and history) and political material. It also publishes political writings from abroad translated into Chinese.

Sanlian Shudian (Joint Publishing Company) is the result of a merger in 1948 of three presses, Life Books, New Knowledge Books and Study Press, founded in the twenties and thirties. It publishes both Chinese and foreign academic writings in philosophy, economics and history.

Number of Publishing Houses in China
(as of December 1980)

Publishing houses at the central level	100
Directly under the State Administration of Publications	12
Under the Party Central Committee departments, the ministries and commissions of the State Council and mass organizations	86
Attached to the People's Liberation Army	2
Publishing houses under the provinces, centrally administered municipalities and autonomous regions	92
Comprehensive	32
Specialized	60
Science and Technology	13
Literature and Art	14
Culture and Education	7
Ethnic Minorities	12
Juvenile	3
Other	11
Total	192

In 1979 it founded the magazine *Dushu* (*Study*) and the series *Renwu* (*Public Figures*).

Shangwu Yinshuguan (Commercial Press) was founded in Shanghai in 1897 to publish dictionaries and reference books in Chinese and other languages. It also edits and translates works on the social sciences from abroad.

Zhonghua Shuju (China Publishing House) was established on January 1, 1912 for the purpose of reprinting traditional Chinese works of literature, history and philosophy.

Renmin Wenxue Chubanshe (People's Literature Press) publishes classical and modern works of literature and literary theory, including works from abroad. It was founded in March 1951.

Waiguo Wenxue Chubanshe (Foreign Literature Press) publishes foreign literary works, with the emphasis on contemporary works. Its range includes theory and research, and it also publishes research by Chinese scholars on foreign literature. It was founded in June 1979.

Renmin Meishu Chubanshe (People's Fine Arts Press) publishes classical and modern fine arts, theoretical studies, new year pictures and cartoon books. It also publishes art from abroad. It was established in September 1951.

Renmin Yinyue Chubanshe (People's Music Press) was founded in 1954 to publish modern, classical and folk music. It also publishes Western classical music as well as technical books.

Zhongguo Dabaike Quanshu Chubanshe (Chinese Encyclopaedia Press) was founded in July 1978. Its main task is to publish the encyclopaedic yearbook of China, a project of the Chinese Encyclopaedia.

Zhishi Chubanshe (Knowledge Books Press) was founded in 1979. Its main purpose is to publish basic knowledge materials and reference works.

Beijing Mangwen Chubanshe (Beijing Braille Press) was founded in December 1978; its purpose is to publish books for the blind.

B. Major Presses Under the Departments of the Party Central Committee and the Ministries and Commissions of the State Council and Mass Organizations:

Renmin Ribao Chubanshe (People's Daily Press) was founded in March 1956. Its main task is to publish the journal of the Party Central Committee, *Renmin Ribao* (*People's Daily*). It also edits and prints books and magazines.

Xinhua Chubanshe (New China Press) was founded in July 1979. Its main task is to publish news and political material.

Gongren Chubanshe (Workers' Press) was founded in July 15, 1949. It is a general publisher with an audience of workers and trade union staff members. It concentrates on theoretical studies on the labour movement and materials connected with the labour movement and trade unions, and also publishes popular political and literary writings designed for workers.

Zhongguo Qingnian Chubanshe (Chinese Youth Press) is a general press with an audience of young people and youth organization staff members. It concentrates on political theory, ideological training, literary works and reading materials on the social and natural sciences. It also publishes magazines and series such as *Zhongguo Qingnian* (*Chinese Youth*), *Hongqi Piaopiao* (*Keep the Red Flag Flying*), *Fudaoyuan* (*The Instructor*) and *Lüxingjia* (*The Traveller*).

Zhongguo Shaonian Ertong Chubanshe (Chinese Children's Press) was founded in October 1955. It is a general press for children and concentrates on children's literature and science books designed for children. It also publishes four magazines, *Zhongxuesheng* (*The Student*), *Women Ai Kexue* (*We Love Science*), *Ertong Wenxue* (*Children's Literature*) and *Zhongguo Ertong* (*Chinese Children*).

Zhongguo Shehui Kexue Chubanshe (Chinese Social Sciences Press) was founded in June 1978. Its main task is to publish books on the social sciences edited and translated by the research institutes of the Chinese Academy of Social Sciences and other research units. It also publishes basic research materials, textbooks, reference works and basic knowledge writings in the social sciences.

Kexue Chubanshe (Science Press) was founded in August 1954. It concentrates on domestic achievements in scientific research, research materials and theoretical works. It also publishes magazines, academic journals, reference books and dictionaries in all of the sciences, as well as Chinese translations of important scientific writings from abroad.

Kexue Puji Chubanshe (Popular Science Press) publishes popular scientific works. It has a branch in Guangzhou.

Zhongguo Xiju Chubanshe (Chinese Theatre Press) was founded in 1957; its purpose is to publish books and periodicals about drama.

Zhongguo Dianying Chubanshe (Chinese Cinema Press) was founded in May 1956. Its main purpose is to publish books on Chinese and foreign films, covering theory, history, scripts, science and technology, illustrations and songs. It also publishes *Dazhong Dianying* (*Popular Cinema*), *Dianying Yishu* (*Film Arts*), *Dianying Juzuo* (*Film Scripts*), *Dianying Jishu* (*Film Technology*), and *Dianying Yishu Yicong* (*Translations on Film Arts*).

Rongbaozhai (Studio of Glorious Treasures) specializes in the reproduction of classical and modern Chinese paintings by water-based printing from wooden plates.

Renmin Jiaoyu Chubanshe (People's Education Press)

was founded in December 1950. It publishes materials for primary, secondary and tertiary education, including teaching programmes, textbooks, reference materials for teachers and theoretical writings on education.

Renmin Weisheng Chubanshe (People's Medical Press) publishes textbooks for medical colleges, reference works and books on popular medicine. It also translates and publishes important medical books from abroad.

Renmin Tiyu Chubanshe (People's Physical Culture Press) was founded in January 1954. Its main purpose is to translate and publish books on physical culture, including theory, history, sports techniques, competition rules, judges' regulations, military physical culture, popular knowledge and textbooks. It also publishes magazines and series such as *Tiyu Keji* (*Physical Culture*), *Tiyu Yiwen* (*Translations on Physical Culture*), *Zuqiu Shijie* (*Football*) and *Tianjing* (*Track and Field*).

Minzu Chubanshe (Minorities Press) was founded in January 1953. Its main task is to translate and publish works by Marx, Engels, Lenin, Stalin and Mao Zedong, and Party and government documents in minority languages, such as Mongolian, Tibetan, Uygur, Kazak and Korean. It also publishes literature and scientific material.

Ditu Chubanshe (Cartographic Press) was founded in 1954. Its main purpose is to publish maps (atlas and wall maps) and books on cartography.

C. Major Publishers in Shanghai:

Shanghai Renmin Chubanshe (Shanghai People's Press) was founded in March 1951 and concentrates on political materials. Its publications include books on politics, law, philosophy, history, Party building and youth training.

It also edits and publishes the magazines and series *Dangde Shenghuo* (*Party Life*), *Qingnian Yidai* (*The Young Generation*), *Shulin* (*Books*) and *Dangshi Ziliao* (*Materials on Party History*).

Shanghai Wenyi Chubanshe (*Shanghai Art and literature Press*) concentrates on literary theory, works of literature, folk literature, drama and film. It also publishes many series and magazines such as *Lu Xun Yanjiu* (*Lu Xun Studies*), *Meixue* (*Aesthetics*) and *Wenyi Lun Cong* (*Literary Series*).

Shanghai Kexue Jishu Chubanshe (Shanghai Scientific and Technological Press) was founded in September 1958. It is a general science and technology press.

Shanghai Cishu Chubanshe (Shanghai Dictionary Press) was founded in January 1978. Its main purpose is to edit and publish all kinds of Chinese language dictionaries.

Shanghai Yiwen Chubanshe (Shanghai Translation Press) was founded in January 1978. It specializes in translating, editing and publishing foreign literature, philosophy, social sciences, and textbooks.

Shanghai Guji Chubanshe (Shanghai Antiquarian Press) was founded in January 1978. Its main function is to publish new editions of classical books.

Shanghai Renmin Meishu Chubanshe (Shanghai People's Fine Arts Press) was founded in August 1952. Its main task is to popularize the fine arts, but it also publishes modern and classical art works from China and abroad and works on art history and theory. It also puts out seven magazines and series on art and photography, such as *Yiyuan Duoying* (*Choice Blossoms from the Garden of Art*), *Meishu Congkan* (*Fine Arts Series*) and *Jiangshan Duo Jiao* (*A Land of Beauty*).

(4) FOREIGN LANGUAGES PUBLISHING

After the founding of the People's Republic of China, increasing international contacts promoted the founding of the China Information Bureau of the Information Administration of the People's Republic of China in Beijing. In 1952 it was organized into the Foreign Languages Press. In 1963 the Foreign Languages Publication and Distribution Bureau was established with the aim of strengthening foreign languages publishings. The bureau controls the editing, translation, publication, printing and distribution of books and magazines. It has two presses and six magazine publishers under its administration.

Waiwen Tushu Chubanshe (Foreign Languages Press) was founded in 1952 as the successor to the China Information Bureau. In a period of over 30 years it has translated and published more than 8,000 books and albums in 43 languages. Its publications include the works of Marx, Engels, Lenin, Stalin and Mao Zedong, Party and government documents, and books on China's economy, literature, art, education and health, with the emphasis on books providing basic and background knowledge of China. The total number of copies printed reaches several hundred millions. At present, it publishes a wide range of books in English, French, Spanish, German, Japanese, Arabic, Korean, Urdu, Hindi, Thai and Bengali.

Xin Shijie Chubanshe (New World Press) publishes books mainly in English about China written by foreigners. Authors whose works it has published since 1951 include Anna Louise Strong, Israel Epstein, Rewi Alley, Jack Chen and Paul Engle. In 1979 it began to publish books in English about China by Chinese authors.

Renmin Huabao She (People's Pictorial Press) was founded in 1950. It publishes a large-format illustrated monthly magazine — known as *Renmin Huabao* (*People's Pictorial*) in China and *Zhongguo Huabao* (*China Pictorial*) abroad. It appears in 19 languages: Chinese, Mongolian, Tibetan, Uygur, Kazak, Korean, Russian, English, German, French, Japanese, Hindi, Spanish, Arabic, Swahili, Swedish, Italian, Urdu and Romanian.

Zhongguo Jianshe Zazhi She (China Reconstructs Press) was founded in 1952 by the China Welfare Institute headed by Soong Ching Ling. It publishes a popular monthly magazine called *Zhongguo Jianshe* (*China Reconstructs*), which appears in Chinese, English, Spanish, French, Arabic, German and Portuguese.

Beijing Zhoubao She (Beijing Review Press) was founded in 1958. Its function is to publish a weekly magazine on politics and current events called *Beijing Zhoubao* (*Beijing Review*), which appears in English, French, Spanish, German and Japanese.

Renmin Zhongguo Zazhi She (People's China Press) was founded in 1950. It publishes a Japanese-language monthly magazine called *Renmin Zhongguo* (*People's China*).

Zhongguo Baodao Zazhi She (Chinese News Magazine Press) was founded in 1950 by the Chinese National Esperanto Association. Its function is to publish a monthly magazine in Esperanto, known as *El Popola Ĉinio* (*People's China*). In 1979 it also began to publish books in Esperanto.

Zhongguo Wenxue Zazhi She (Chinese Literature Press) was founded in 1951. It publishes a monthly journal in English on Chinese literature and art (including criticism and theory), called *Zhongguo Wenxue* (*Chinese Litera-*

ture). There is also a French edition, which appears quarterly. It also publishes translations from Chinese literature in a new series, Panda Books.

The majority of foreign language books and periodicals in China are published by the presses under the Foreign Languages Publication and Distribution Bureau. Other foreign language periodicals published in China include *Women of China, China's Foreign Trade, China's Sports, The Chinese Medical Journal, Scientia Sinica, Science Bulletin, Social Sciences in China* and *China's Screen.*

Number of Books Published in China 1949-80

Year	Books	Copies printed (in ten thousand)
1949	8,000	10,500
1956	28,773	178,437
1957	27,571	127,544
1965	20,143	217,148
1966	11,055	349,645
1970	4,889	187,649
1976	12,842	291,399
1979	17,212	407,178
1980	21,621	459,298
Total 1949-80		6,294,846

Book Publication in 1980

Type	Books	Number of copies (in ten thousand)
General	15,669	191,013
Philosophy, politics, economics and history	2,091	31,942
Culture and education	2,095	54,949
Literature and art	3,322	25,765
Nature, science and technology	5,715	22,861
Children's books	2,446	55,496
Textbooks	3,440	189,515
College and secondary specialized school textbooks	1,599	6,633
Secondary and primary level textbooks	1,207	172,246
Part-time education textbooks	175	5,463
Teachers' aides	459	5,173
Picture books and albums	2,512	78,770
Total	21,621	459,298

4. PRINTING AND DISTRIBUTION

(1) PRINTING

China is the first country where printing was invented,

but prolonged feudal rule delayed its further development. Modern printing in China dates only from the turn of the century, when foreign machines were imported into China. Before Liberation the printing industry consisted mainly of a few printing machine repair shops in the coastal cities, which could only produce medium and small-sized printing machines — larger ones had to be imported from abroad. The printing industry was almost non-existent in the inland cities and border areas, especially in ethnic minority areas.

The development of the printing industry since the founding of New China has been quite rapid. The first step was to the merger of privately owned printing shops (which accounted for 96 per cent of the national printing industry) with state-owned printing shops, so that the whole industry became a socialist, state-owned one. Secondly, new printing shops were set up. For instance, important printeries set up in the Beijing area in the early years of the People's Republic include the Xinhua Printing House, the Fine Arts Printing House (which published *People's Pictorial*), the Foreign Languages Printing House and the Ethnic Minorities Printing House. Printing houses were also set up in Shenyang, Hankou, Xi'an and Chongqing. After 1956, technical workers and cadres from Shanghai and Beijing were sent to border areas to strengthen the printing industry there by founding or expanding existing printing shops. Colour printing can now be done in many provinces, and most counties have their own printing shops. Thirdly, by 1979, 53 printing machine factories have been built or expanded in 21 of the 29 provinces, centrally administered municipalities and autonomous regions, including Beijing, Shanghai, Shaanxi, Hunan, Zhejiang and Shandong. According to 1979 statistics, 160,000 printing machines of 153 types have been manufactured. At the end of 1980, there were 198 printing shops in China (not including newspaper and other specialized printeries) with 130,000 printing workers and staff members. The capacity for printing books and periodicals (measured in reams of paper) was 31 times that in the first years after Liberation (670,000 reams). Fourthly, the scientific research in printing techniques and the training of printing workers has been improved. China's first technical research institute for printing was established in 1956 in Beijing, followed soon after by another in Shanghai. At present printing and binding technical research institutes exist in Beijing, Tianjin, Liaoning, Hunan, Guangdong, Yunnan and Shaanxi. A printing college was set up in 1978. Technical schools and courses for training printers also exist in Beijing, Shanghai, Hunan, Guangdong, Guangxi and Yunnan. These research institutes, colleges, schools and courses have produced a large quantity of qualified personnel in the printing industry. Fifthly, the production of the materials needed in printing is basically in the hands of the industry itself. In order to improve the production and supply of printing machines, the Chinese Printing Machinery Company was set up in 1958.

At present China's major printing methods include letterpress, offset, intaglio, three-colour copperplate, collotype, silk screen and woodblock printing. Letterpress printing is the most common. Offset printing is mostly confined to illustrations, pictorials, posters and postcards.

Intaglio is only used in a few printing shops in Beijing, Shanghai and Guangdong. Offset printing is preferred to three-colour copperplate printing in most printing shops because of the latter's complicated plate making and high production cost. Collotype is only used for books in archaeology and art. Silk screen printing is a fairly recent innovation. Traditional Chinese woodblock printing was on the way out before Liberation, but now has been revived on a large scale. The woodblock-printed art reproductions made by Rongbaozhai in Beijing and Duoyunxuan Arts Studio in Shanghai are highly regarded at home and abroad.

(2) DISTRIBUTION

Since its founding the Chinese Communist Party has attached great importance to the publication and distribution of books and magazines. After Liberation the distribution of books and periodicals was brought under a central administration. A general administrative office of the Xinhua Bookstore was founded in Beijing in October 1949, with three departments attached to it: publication, printing and distribution. At that time there were 735 branches of the Xinhua Bookstore throughout the country, which also handled publication, printing and distribution. In January 1951 these comprehensive branches became outlets for distribution only. The distribution network was then strengthened. In 1980 there were 5,321 Xinhua bookstores in China, plus 60,000

The Xinhua News Agency, the
largest news agency in China.

Chinese TV stations sponsor regular educational programmes. Seen here is a medical lecture transmitted by the Shanghai open TV university.

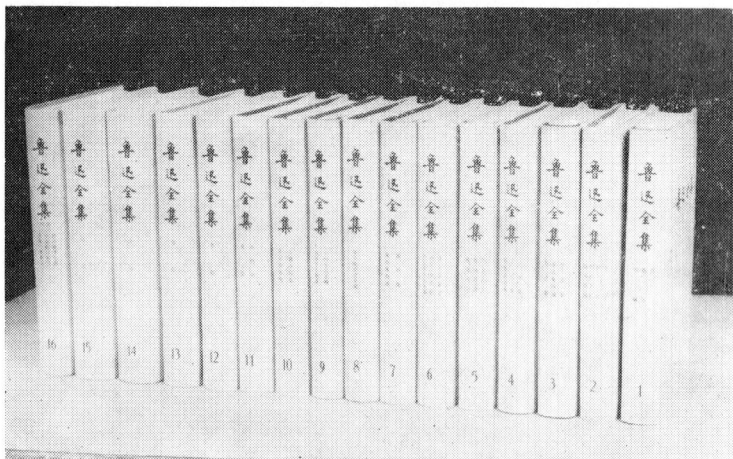

The 16-volume *Complete Works of Lu Xun*, published in 1981 in commemoration of the centenary of the birth of the great Chinese writer.

Books in foreign languages published in recent years by the Foreign Languages Press.

Beijing Library, the largest library in China.

A reading room in Beijing Library.

Recreational and sports activities figure prominently in the programmes regularly organized by cultural centres in rural areas.

Heshun Library in Tengchong County, Yunnan Province. The largest rural library in the country, it has a collection of more than 40,000 volumes and holds subscriptions to 20 newspapers and more than 60 magazines.

Children's centres sponsor regular scientific programmes and recreational and sports activities tailored to children's needs.

The Peking Man Exhibition Hall at Zhoukoudian.

A cave at Zhoukoudian in the southwestern suburbs of Beijing, where the fossils of Peking Man who lived 500,000 years ago were found.

Banpo Village, a site of the 7,000-year-old Yangshao Culture, in Xi'an, Shaanxi.

A museum at the Banpo Village site.

The Museum of Qin Shi Huang's Buried Legion Sculpture. It is built over the three underground vaults excavated on the east side of the mausoleum of Emperor Qin Shi Huang of the Qin Dynasty (r. 246-210 B.C.) on the northern foothills of Lishan Mountain in Lintong, Shaanxi.

Life-size figures of warriors
and chariots in the museum.

The Hall of Supreme Harmony in the former imperial palace of the Ming and Qing dynasties (1368-1911) in Beijing. It is where grand ceremonies were held, such as the accession of a new emperor to the throne, the reception of ministers by the emperor, and the celebration of festivals. The Palace Museum in the imperial palace is one of the largest and oldest state museums in China.

agents in rural department stores. The distribution
network now extends into all parts of China. In 1950
there were only 12,000 workers and staff members
employed in Xinhua bookstores and the turnover was
200,000,000 copies. In 1980 there were 66,868 workers
and staff members and the turnover amounted to 4,250
million copies. Turnover therefore increased by 21 times
over the 1950 figure. According to statistics, the total
number of volumes distributed between 1950 and 1980
was 67,600 million, and total sales amounted to 14,450
million yuan.

The Xinhua bookstores are the major distributors of all
books published in China. Newspapers and periodicals are
distributed through the post office by subscriptions or
direct sales. Some of the Xinhua bookstores also handle
single copy sales of periodicals. At present almost 50,000
post office branches or agencies which distribute newspapers and periodicals, plus several hundred thousand offices or agents in basic-level units accept subscriptions on
behalf of the post office.

The Xinhua Bookstore Head Office in Beijing is the
administration organ for the domestic distribution of
books. It is attached to the State Administration of
Publications. Each of the provinces, centrally administered
municipalities and autonomous regions has a Xinhua office to run the branch bookstores. The branch stores in
cities and counties sell books directly. For instance there
are 50 branches in the city districts of Beijing, all under
the Beijing Xinhua Bookstore. The Wangfujing Bookstore
in the centre of Beijing is one of the largest in the country
and handles more than 20,000 customers daily. Each

province, centrally administered municipality and autonomous region also has specialized bookstores selling foreign
language, science and antiquarian books. There are altogether 29 foreign language bookstores throughout the
country (not including Tibet).

Foreign language books are distributed by the China
Publications Centre (Guoji Shudian), Zhongguo Chuban
Duiwai Maoyi Zonggongsi (Chinese National Publications
Foreign Trade Company) and Zhongguo Tushu Jinchukou
Zonggongsi (Chinese National Publications Import and
Export Coorporation).

The China Publications Centre was founded in Beijing
in December 1949 to handle the import and export of
books and periodicals. It was under the State Publications Bureau and later the Commission for Cultural
Relations with Foreign Countries. In September 1963 it
was transferred to the Foreign Languages Publication and
Distribution Bureau.

The China Publications Centre now handles mainly
books, periodicals and newspapers in Chinese and foreign
languages, original paintings and reproductions, paper-
cuts, bookmarks, gramophone records and tapes. Since
1949 it has distributed tens of thousands of books, including 8,000 titles of all kinds in over 40 foreign languages.
In 1979, more than 330 newspapers and magazines were
distributed in more than 170 countries and regions. Its
total distribution in 1979 amounted to more than
28,040,000 copies, including 11,000,000 copies of newspapers and periodicals. In the same year, it also published
more than 400 books in 19 languages in co-operation with
foreign publishers.

Book Distribution 1950-80

Year	Number of copies sold (in ten thousand)	Sales (in 10,000 yuan)
1950	20,000	4,500
1956	147,814	30,189
1957	129,698	28,354
1966	357,709	48,498
1972	199,474	40,132
1976	340,908	66,829
1979	378,610	126,103
1980	425,314	154,965
Total 1950-80	6,748,190	1,443,441

Chapter Two

LIBRARIES, COMMUNITY CULTURAL CENTRES AND WORKERS' CULTURAL CENTRES

1. LIBRARIES

(1) A BRIEF HISTORY OF CHINESE LIBRARIES

Ancient libraries Four kinds of libraries existed in ancient China, official, private, college and monastic. They were known generally as *cang shu lou*, or "book repositories".

Official libraries catered exclusively to members of the ruling house, officials and aristocrats. They began to take shape in the reign of Emperor Chengdi of the Han Dynasty more than 2,000 years ago, when a special archive was set up by the court and the noted scholar Liu Xiang (79-8 B.C.) was assigned to rearrange and collate the royal collections. After his death, he was succeeded by his son, Liu Xin, who compiled a catalogue of the collections classified into seven categories giving brief introductions to each category. Known as the *Qi Lue* (*Seven Summaries*), it is the earliest national library catalogue in China.

The number of libraries increased rapidly with the invention of paper and printing. Among them the best-known were the Guangwendian (Reading Hall) of the Sui Dynasty (581-618), the Hongwenguan (Erudition Hall) of the Tang (618-907), the Chongwenyuan (Respect for Learning Court) of the Song (960-1279), the Hongwenyuan (Erudition Court) of the Yuan (1271-1368), the Wenyuange (Pavilion of Learning) of the Ming (1368-1644), and the official libraries of the Qing Dynasty (1644-1911) in the Forbidden City and the Yuanmingyuan in Beijing and in Chengde, Liaoning, Zhenjiang, Yangzhou and Hangzhou. Due to government financing, secure organization and specialized staff, official libraries generally had larger collections and ranged wider than private ones.

Most of the private libraries belonged to landlords, officials or scholars. The names of more than 1,100 famous collectors, from the Song to the Qing Dynasty, are on record. Private collectors not only bought and collected books but hand-copied them, prepared critical editions, made wood-block prints and wrote books themselves. Mao Zijin of the Ming Dynasty had a collection exceeding 84,000 fascicles in his private library, the Jiguge (Ancient Collection Pavilion), and block-printed *Annotations to the Thirteen Classics*, *The Seventeen Histories* and *Anthology of Song and Yuan Poetry and Prose*. By the Qing Dynasty, the number of books in the hands of private collectors had surpassed that of official libraries. Most of the private collectors were in Jiangsu and Zhejiang, followed by Hunan, Guangdong, Sichuan and Shandong. Yang Yizeng of Liaocheng, Shandong, was the most famous book collector in north China, known especially for his collection of rare Song and Yuan block-printed editions. Qu Yong of Changshu, Jiangsu, led the collectors in south China in Song and Yuan editions. Although individual private collectors had smaller collections than official libraries, they concentrated mostly on rare books. Because they were scattered throughout various parts of the country, their collections benefited a much wider circle of readers, including their families, relatives and friends. Private collectors, therefore, had a distinct role in the spread of culture.

The *shu yuan*, or colleges, first appeared in the Tang Dynasty as places where scholars and men of letters could meet for learned discussions, and many of them had libraries of their own. Among the most well-known were the Donglin College in the Tang Dynasty and the Bailu, Yuelu, Yingtian and Songyang colleges in the Song Dynasty, all with large collections of books. The *shu yuan* later developed to become educational institutions within the old-style civil examination system. In the Qing Dynasty, there were *shu yuan* in practically all provinces, prefectures and counties. Most of them had their own libraries containing large quantities of the classics, which were the prescribed texts for the civil examinations.

Monastic collections were an important part of book collecting in ancient China. Since Buddhism and Taoism played a major role in traditional social life, many of the well-known Buddhist and Taoist temples had their own collections consisting mostly of Buddhist and Taoist classics.

Modern libraries Between the late 19th century and the early 20th century, Chinese bourgeois reformists began to establish modern schools, newspapers and translation offices. At the same time they also set up a number of public libraries, notably the Qiangxuehui (Self-Strengthening Study Society) Book Repository in Shanghai, the Nanxuehui (South China Study Society) Book Repository in Guangzhou, and the Guyue Book Repository in Zhejiang. Apart from the Chinese classics, these libraries also contained political, economic, literary and scientific books and journals from the West. After the abortive Reform Movement of 1898, the Qing government switched to a moderate policy and established public libraries, using for the first time the modern term *tushuguan*, or "library". The best-known among the earliest public libraries were the Jiangnan Library and the Metropolitan Library opened in 1907 and 1910. On the eve of the Revolution of 1911, there were 18 public libraries in the country, some of them run by provincial authorities. The colleges were remodelled along modern lines and their book repositories changed into affiliated school libraries. The Metropolitan University Library, founded in 1902, was the best-known school library.

Public libraries experienced further expansion after the 1911 Revolution, when county and town libraries and newspaper reading rooms began to appear. The Metropolitan Popular Library established in 1914 in Beijing had a dozen branch public reading rooms. In 1916, there were 239 popular libraries and 1,803 public newspaper reading rooms throughout the country, whose clientele extended from feudal scholar-officials to bourgeois and petty-bourgeois intellectuals.

Around the time of the May 4 Movement of 1919, new cultural organizations sprang up like mushrooms after rain. With them came the appearance of many new, progressive libraries, such as the Marxist Study Society Library set up by Li Dazhao and Deng Zhongxia in the early 1920s and the Cultural Club Library and Hunan Independent Study University Library set up by Mao Zedong in Changsha, Hunan. The Tongxin Library in Shanghai had the greatest influence and lasted longest. It extended its service to large cities in 20 provinces as well as to overseas Chinese in Southeast Asia, Japan, the United States and France until it was closed down by the Kuomintang government in 1929. With the spread of the workers' movement following the birth of the Chinese Communist Party in 1921, a number of libraries for ordinary people appeared, notably the Tianjin Workers' Library, founded in 1922, the Tangshan Workers' Library and the Nanchang People's Library. Other influential progressive libraries include the Mayi Library and the *Shenbao Daily* Affiliated Library, both in Shanghai during the 1930s. Although limited in number and size and soon prohibited by the Kuomintang government, these libraries played a significant role in establishing the principle that libraries should meet the needs of the common people. In response to the initial expansion of libraries in the country, a national librarians' federation was formed in 1925 under the name of the Chinese National Library Association. By 1936, the number of libraries in China had reached 5,196. During the Japanese war of aggression against China (1937-45), many of the country's valuable books and cultural treasures were vandalized, while the number of libraries in Kuomintang-controlled areas decreased from 5,196 to 1,178 in 1938 and then to 940 in 1943. The situation further deteriorated when the Kuomintang government unleashed the nationwide civil war after the anti-Japanese war, so that only 391 libraries remained in existence on the eve of Liberation, and only 55 were public libraries above county level. These libraries were inadequately financed, poorly stocked (totalling about 26.89 million volumes) and concentrated in large cities and coastal regions, leaving the vast rural areas and remote regions a wasteland in this respect.

(2) LIBRARIES IN NEW CHINA

After national Liberation, the People's Government took over the public libraries from the Kuomintang government and brought private libraries under state planning. Establishing the principle of serving workers, peasants and soldiers, the government stocked libraries with the Marxist classics and progressive books and journals, made regulations concerning the supply of publications, rationally readjusted the geographical distribution of libraries by reorganizing old libraries and setting up new ones, increased the construction of libraries in inland and remote regions as well as in factories, rural areas and city communities, and trained specialized library personnel. In 1980, there were upwards of 300,000 libraries of different types throughout the country within a comprehensive, rationally distributed network. Government allocations for books in 1979 was 40 per cent more than in 1976 and continued to increase in 1980. A Library Administrative Bureau has been set up under the Ministry of Culture to strengthen leadership in library work.

Public libraries   The backbone of the country's library network, public libraries have experienced a rapid expansion in the past three decades or more. There were 1,732 public libraries above the county level in 1980, as against 55 on the eve of Liberation, and their total collection has increased from 16 million to 210 million volumes.

Public libraries in China exist at each of the three administrative divisions and are generally located in the political or cultural centres of these administrative divisions. In addition to the national library in Beijing, there are public libraries at the level of provinces, central-administered municipalities and autonomous regions, the administrative regions and cities, and the city districts and counties.

Beijing Library, the national library in Beijing that succeeded the Metropolitan Library of the late Qing Dynasty, was opened to the public in 1912. In 1980, it had a collection of 10 million volumes, or more than seven times the figure of 1.45 million in 1949. It held subscriptions to 13,000 Chinese and foreign magazines and 3,600 newspapers, and foreign publications in 115 languages. Its book collection includes many rare and valuable items, such as a hand-written copy of the *Buddhist Admonitions* of the Northern Wei Dynasty (A.D. 458), and 280,000 hand-written and block-printed copies of the Song, Jin, Yuan, Ming and Qing dynasties, including a hand-copied *Yongle Encyclopaedia* dating from the Ming Dynasty and a hand-copied *Complete Library of the Four Treasuries of Knowledge* from the Qing Dynasty. It also holds photographs, maps, rubbings from inscriptions on ancient bronzes and stone tablets, oracle bones, manuscripts of famous writers, microfilms and microfiches. Beijing Library is the national deposit library and also the centre of interlibrary loans and cataloguing, and is responsible for coordination between libraries all over the country. Internationally, it is a deposit centre for United Nations publications and an exchange centre for foreign books and periodicals. By 1980, it had established exchange relations with more than 2,000 organizations in 120 countries and regions and interlibrary loans with libraries in several countries. Because facilities in the present Beijing Library are outdated and the floor space of its storage and reading rooms is limited, a plan was made in 1979 for the construction of a new complex on a new site.

At the provincial, municipal or autonomous regional

level there are 31 libraries, most of them with a collection exceeding a million volumes. They are centres for the purchase and cataloguing of books and serials, and for interlibrary loans and professional research for their provinces, municipalities or autonomous regions. The following 26 libraries have collections which exceeded one million volumes in 1979:

Name	Location	Date Founded	Collection (in ten thousand volumes)
Capital Library	Beijing	1913	195
Tianjin Municipal People's Library	Tianjin	1952	260
Shanghai Municipal Library	Shanghai	1952	692
Liaoning Provincial Library	Shenyang	1946	212
Jilin Provincial Library	Changchun	1960	212
Heilongjiang Provincial Library	Harbin	1958	160
Shanxi Provincial Library	Taiyuan	1957	146
Inner Mongolian Library	Hohhot	1950	112
Shandong Provincial Library	Jinan	1908	286

Name	Location	Date Founded	Collection (in ten thousand volumes)
Jiangxi Provincial Library	Nanchang	1928	150
Fujian Provincial Library	Fuzhou	1929	155
Anhui Provincial Library	Hefei	1953	132
Zhejiang Provincial Library	Hangzhou	1903	225
Nanjing Library	Nanjing	1933	490
Sun Yat-sen Library, Guangdong	Guangzhou	1922	232
Guangxi Zhuang Autonomous Regional Library No. 2	Nanning	1954	111
Hunan Provincial Library	Changsha	1912	256
Hubei Provincial Library	Wuhan	1904	191
Henan Provincial Library	Zhengzhou	1950	150
Shaanxi Provincial Library	Xi'an	1909	183
Gansu Provincial Library	Lanzhou	1916	183

Name	Location	Date Founded	Collection (in ten thousand volumes)
Qinghai Provincial Library	Xining	1935	129
Ningxia Hui Autonomous Regional Library	Yinchuan	1958	109
Sichuan Provincial Library	Chengdu	1940	285
Guizhou Provincial Library	Guiyang	1937	106
Yunnan Provincial Library	Kunming	1919	160

There are 243 libraries at the administrative region or city level, of which 11 have a collection exceeding half a million volumes, and 1,457 libraries at the city district or county level. Maintaining direct ties with the masses in the towns and rural areas, these major libraries at the basic level stock mainly popular works in science, technology, the classics and literature for readers with an intermediate education, and follow the principle of popularization and education with the emphasis on popularization. Apart from their regular opening hours, they extend their services to villages and basic-level units through mobile lending stations. They also give guidance to library work in rural communes and production brigades.

College and university libraries These have a fairly long history and solid foundations in China, and have

undergone further growth with the rapid progress of
higher education after Liberation. In 1956, there were
225 college libraries, with a total of 8.898 million volumes,
compared with 132 with a total of 7.94 million volumes in
1950. According to the statistics of April 1981, there
were 670 college libraries, with a total of 200 million
volumes or more and a staff of 17,000 (as against 3,000
in the 1950s). Of these, 35 had a collection exceeding one million volumes, including Beijing University
Library, which had more than three million volumes,
and the libraries of Zhongshan University, Nanjing
University, the Chinese People's University and the
Beijing Teachers' University, which had upwards of
two million volumes each. Apart from having better-
quality collections, the libraries of the institutions of
higher learning have a fairly systematic and comprehensive book stock geared to the needs of their departments
and disciplines, and their large quantities of foreign
language publications have a much wider circulation than
in other libraries. In addition to administrative divisions
for acquisitions, circulation, the classics and reading rooms
for private study, many of the college libraries have
special academic reference departments for the acquisition, administration and distribution of new domestic and
foreign reference materials, and most of them have reference rooms in the departments and research units to
assist teaching and scientific research.

Scientific and technological libraries These have been
set up along specialized lines to provide direct service to
scientific research and technological studies. They include the libraries of the departments under the Chinese
Academy of Sciences, the research institutes under the
government ministries and large mines and factories as

well as specialized libraries. Many of them have established exchange relations with their foreign counterparts and therefore have more new scientific works, journals and reference materials than libraries of other types. Each of the specialized academic fields in the country has its own fairly comprehensive collection of publications. The Chinese Academy of Sciences Library, the Chinese Academy of Medical Sciences Library, the Chinese Academy of Agricultural Sciences Library, the Chinese National Geological Library, the Chinese Medical Research Academy Library and other national specialized libraries are the central libraries in their respective fields. Such libraries have expanded rapidly in the past three decades or more. In 1950, for instance, there were only 17 libraries attached to the department in the Chinese Academy of Sciences, with a total of 630,000 volumes, whereas the number grew to 101 with a total of 5.5 million volumes in 1957 and to more than 150 with a total of 12 million volumes and a staff of 2,000 in 1980. Thus, a comprehensive library network has taken shape in the Chinese Academy of Sciences, composed of the libraries of its headquarters, its provincial branches and its research institutes.

Trade union libraries   They are run by the trade unions at all levels for workers and staff and their families. In the early period of the People's Republic there were 44 trade union libraries. In 1955 the First National Working Conference of Trade Union Libraries decided on the policy of serving the needs of basic-level units, production and the masses. In 1956, the number of trade union libraries increased to 15,438, of which 14,604 were run by trade unions at the basic level. Statistics for June 1980 are given below:

	Number of libraries	Collection of books (in ten thousand volumes)	Number of full-time staff
Total	108,882	22,509.9	30,998
Libraries run by trade unions above the basic level	2,898	1,322.9	2,106
Libraries run by trade unions at the basic level	105,984	21,187	28,892

At present, a trade union library network organized according to industry and a regional trade union library network centred on factories or enterprises are taking shape.

Children's libraries   Children's libraries in China fall into four main categories. 1) The nine large children's libraries run by the state, such as the Beijing Children's Library, the Shanghai Children's Library and the Tianjin Children's Library. 2) The 590 children's reading rooms attached to public libraries throughout China. 3) The children's libraries or reading rooms in children's centres or clubs. 4) Libraries or reading rooms in primary and secondary schools, which specialize in books on general and scientific knowledge and moral education. In coordination with schools they also sponsor a wide range of activities, such as reading programmes, forums and discussions.   School libraries are small in number (many of the rural primary and secondary schools do not have libraries) and their collections are insignificant. This problem became an item in the agenda of a national children's library work conference held in 1981.

City community libraries and rural libraries City community libraries or reading rooms run by neighbourhoods cater directly to city residents, and their collections comprise mainly popular primers. Though poorly stocked and equipped, they have a mass reading public that consists mostly of retired workers and staff, school leavers waiting for employment, and school children. These libraries also offer their services to the increasing number of neighbourhood-run factories and enterprises and private shops.

Most of the rural libraries or reading rooms were set up after the birth of the People's Republic, especially during the movement for co-operative farming, and are housed in the cultural centres of the communes or production brigades.

Interlibrary co-operation In 1957, the Scientific Planning Commission under the State Council set up a Library Section to coordinate the work of libraries throughout the country. Later, it established two national central library committees, in Beijing and Shanghai, and nine regional central library committees, in Shenyang, Wuhan, Guangzhou, Nanjing, Chengdu, Xi'an, Tianjin, Lanzhou and Harbin. Coordination committees or central library committees were also set up in some of the provinces. Under unified, overall planning and management, interlibrary co-operation was effected with great success in the purchase of foreign language publications, the allocation of books, the compilation of union catalogues and the training of library personnel. The National Union Catalogue Compilation Board formed in the early 1960s, for example, turned out upwards of 300 union catalogues and periodically published National Western Language Accessions Lists. This nationwide coordination was suspended in the "cultural revolution" and has been resumed only in recent years. Between 1976 and 1979, a group of over 400 organizations led by the Chinese Institute of Scientific and Technological Information and Beijing Library compiled *A Chinese Character Subject Chart* designed for computer control of subject indices of printed volumes and materials, which has 108,000 entries in various disciplines and fields. Beginning from 1978, a general catalogue of ancient Chinese rare books has been under preparation on a nationwide scale. The completion of this multi-volumed union catalogue will contribute to the knowledge and utilization of China's cultural heritage and cultural exchange. Interlibrary coordination has developed in the past two years. In 1981, a National College and University Library Committee was formed, followed shortly after by the establishment of college and university central library committees in the provinces.

Training of library personnel There are more than 100,000 full-time library staff members throughout China; some are university graduates in library or information science, but most have received in-service training or attended extension courses in librarianship. Part-time staff is also employed.

From 1949 to 1979, China turned out more than 2,000 graduates from the library science departments of universities and more than 1,250 from correspondence universities. There are more than 20 universities with library science departments, offering courses to a total of more than 2,000 students. These include Beijing, Wuhan, Nanjing, Fudan, Hunan and Shanxi universities, the East

China Teachers' University, the Jilin Teachers' University and the Inner Mongolia Teachers' College.

Short-term training courses are the main form of library science education, attracting over half a million people in the past three decades. In addition, many library staff members have received in-service training in extension courses on library science.

The study of library science and library science research societies Library science has developed since Liberation into a special field of study. Achievements have already been made in basic theory, cataloguing, classification systems, the history of Chinese libraries and bibliography. In 1979 the China Library Science Research Society was established with branch societies at the provincial, municipal and autonomous regional level and has since conducted academic seminars. The formation of these societies marks the beginning of a systematic study of library science. There has also been a rapid increase in the publication of books and journals in the field. In 1980, there were more than 20 such journals, such as *Library News* (Journal of the China Library Science Research Society), *Beijing Library Bulletin* (edited by Beijing Library) and *Library Information* (edited by the Chinese Academy of Sciences Library).

2. COMMUNITY ART AND CULTURAL CENTRES

Art and cultural centres are government-run organizations for the popularizing of culture and science and the promotion of cultural activities among the masses. Between 1949 and the early 1960s, a nationwide cultural

network was formed, composed of community art centres
in provinces, central-administered municipalities and
autonomous regions, cultural centres in cities, prefectures
and counties, cultural clubs in city districts and communes, and cultural halls in production brigades. During
the "cultural revolution", these organizations were closed
down and their activities banned. Not until 1976 were
these organizations restored and their activities resumed.
Since then, the number of art and cultural centres and
lower-level organizations has increased rapidly, drawing
in more and more people. In the past two years, cultural
affairs departments have strengthened their leadership
over cultural activities in the countryside and have established cultural centres in some of the small towns and
communes on a trial basis. The chart below shows the
development of the community cultural organizations at
various levels since the founding of the People's Republic:

	Community art centres	Cultural centres	Cultural clubs
1949		896	
1957	39	2,748	2,417
1965	62	2,598	2,087
1979	144	2,892	22,304
1980	218	2,912	25,000

Cultural centres Cultural centres exist in practically all the centrally administered municipalities, districts of the provincially administered cities, and counties. Most of them have their own cinemas, performance halls, recreation rooms, television or lantern slide rooms, libraries and film projection teams. The tasks of the cultural centres are: 1) To propagate the policies and laws of the government and achievements in socialist construction, educate the people in patriotism, socialism and communist morality, and popularize science and culture through sponsoring a wide choice of activities, such as theatrical performances, exhibitions, forums, book and magazine lending services, cultural and scientific studies, and television, lantern slide and film shows; and 2) to guide leisure-time community cultural activities, train cultural centre staff and amateur writers and artists, supply materials for mass entertainments, organize rural cultural work teams to spread culture among peasants, and collect and collate folk art data. These government-financed cultural centres have their own full-time staff and charge a small fee for their programmes to defray costs.

Cultural clubs and halls These are the basic-level organizations for community cultural activities in city neighbourhoods and in rural people's communes. The great majority of clubs are in the communes. Some of these are wholly government-financed, some are run by communes with government aid, and some are wholly financed by communes out of their collective funds. At present one out of every three communes has a cultural club.

Cultural clubs also exist in some of the larger and more prosperous production brigades where the population is relatively dense. They are financed either entirely by the brigades out of their welfare funds or, where welfare funds are insufficient, partly by the Communist Youth League members and other young people out of the proceeds of volunteer labour. Some of the clubs have their own amateur theatrical troupes, rediffusion broadcasting stations, libraries, night schools and film projection teams.

Since China has a rural population of more than 800 million people, the countryside is the focus of current developments in community cultural activities. To strengthen rural cultural work, the state has set the goal of gradually transforming small towns and people's communes into local cultural centres on the basis of existing clubs or halls. In the past two years, by relying on the strength of the collective economy and making use of whatever is available, many communes and market towns have built simplified cinemas, libraries, exhibition halls, recreation rooms, sports grounds and other facilities, and improved the management of their existing facilities. In 1980, more than 100 cultural centres were set up in small towns in Heilongjiang, and it is estimated that rural cultural centres will have been set up in half of the people's communes by 1985.

Neighbourhood cultural clubs or halls in the cities are run by neighbourhood committees with government subsidies for the purchase of books, television sets and other small-scale facilities. They have made their importance increasingly felt with the rise in the number of school leavers waiting for employment, retired workers and staff, and small factories and shops run by neighbourhoods or private investments.

Community art centres These are facilities which offer professional guidance and study for community activities in the arts. Their main tasks are: 1) To give training and guidance to the staff of cultural centres and amateur artists and supply materials for their activities; 2) to collect, edit and present traditional ethnic and folk arts; and 3) to study the development and pattern of community art activities.

Art centres exist at two levels. There are 29 at the provincial, centrally administered municipality or autonomous regional level, and 189 at the special regional or provincially administered city level. The development of such centres since the "cultural revolution" has been fairly rapid.

Governmental mass culture administrative organs The Mass Culture Administrative Bureau in the Ministry of Culture is in charge of national mass cultural work, and similar departments exist at each level in administrative divisions throughout the country.

These organs provide guidance to community cultural work mainly through conducting investigations, publishing journals, sponsoring theatrical festivals, convening meetings, issuing documents and organizing exchanges of experience. The Mass Culture Administrative Bureau publishes a periodical named *Mass Culture* for the exchange of information and experience, and similar journals are published in some provinces and cities. Since 1979, peasants' amateur art festivals and workers' amateur folk ballad festivals have been held at the national and provincial, municipal or autonomous regional levels to compare notes and promote mass cultural activities in urban and rural areas.

3.　WORKERS' CULTURAL CENTRES AND CLUBS

Workers' clubs before Liberation　Workers' clubs, run by trade unions for the cultural enrichment of workers, first appeared in China in the early 1920s.　The most important of the early clubs were the Changxindian Workers' Club in Beijing, the Shanghai Workers' Club and the Jiang'an Railway Workers' Club in Wuhan, all founded in 1921, and the Anyuan Railway and Mining Workers' Club in Jiangxi, founded in 1922.　Many of the leaders of the Chinese Communist Party made important contributions to the initiation and formation of the workers' clubs.

Led by the Communist Party, workers' clubs before Liberation played an important role in organizing workers to read and write, protecting workers' immediate interests, enhancing their class consciousness and opposing imperialism and the reactionary government.

Growth of workers' cultural centres and clubs in New China　After the founding of the People's Republic, the government set up large, well-equipped workers' cultural centres (literally, cultural palaces) in a number of big cities.　Some were housed in architectural landmarks, such as the Imperial Ancestral Temple in Beijing, a gambling den formerly run by an Italian in Tianjin and the private garden of the notorious warlord Yuan Shikai, also in Tianjin. The Trade Union Law promulgated in 1950 specified that the government organs at all levels should allocate to the All-China Federation of Trade Unions, industrial unions and local trade unions the necessary buildings and facilities to enable them to carry out their office work and recreational and welfare activities.　The First National Conference on the Work of Trade Union Clubs convened by the All-China Federation of Trade Unions that year discussed and adopted the regulations concerning the organization and work of the clubs. The number of workers' cultural centres and clubs then increased rapidly throughout the country. In 1955, the Second National Conference on the Work of Trade Union Clubs was held, which further stressed the educational role of the clubs and the principle of serving the needs of basic-level units, production and the masses. The cultural centres and clubs played an increasingly active role. Workers' folk ballads, music and dance festivals, amateur art exhibitions and worker-composers' song competitions were held, giving a great impetus to the workers' clubs. On the eve of the "cultural revolution", many cities had an initial, three-level network for workers' cultural activities, based on the city cultural centres and reaching to clubs in the city districts (and counties) and to factories and mines.

The "cultural revolution" wrought great havoc in regard to workers' cultural activities, which were resumed and became popular again only in recent years. The following chart shows this expansion of workers' cultural centres and clubs:

The number of full-time staff of workers' cultural centres and clubs has grown to 37,630 and that of amateur enthusiasts to 2.59 million, forming a dedicated contingent for mass cultural work. In 1980, 9.4 million people attended activities at the Beijing Working People's Cultural Centre and 22 million attended the 12 district workers' cultural centres and clubs in Shanghai. The cultural centres and clubs, however, are still too small in number to meet the needs of the country's 100 million workers and staff: each of them now caters to an average of 8,200 persons, or more than six times as many as in

	Total	Cultural centres and clubs run by trade unions at all levels	Cultural centres and clubs run by factories and mines
1950	789	16	773
1953	8,355	1,699	6,656
1963	16,901	1,596	15,305
1979	12,142	1,326	10,816
1980	14,717	1,505	13,212

1954. This shortage is even more keenly felt in remote regions and small towns. To solve this problem, while the government has continued to make allocations for building new cultural centres and clubs, local trade unions have set about building their own recreational facilities. Factories and mines in small towns have also pooled their funds for the same purpose.

The activities of the workers' cultural centres and clubs These consist mainly of the following: 1) The organization of scientific-technological and business management study classes, lectures and forums. By 1980, more than 4.9 million workers and staff had attended technical training classes of various types. In 1980, the Beijing Working People's Cultural Centre conducted accounting, industrial statistics and business accounting classes and more than 100 study sessions for workers of the light and textile industries, with an attendance of 11,000. That same year, it admitted 450,000 people to its scientific-technological activities. 2) The encouragement of worker-staff participation in amateur art and literary activities. Local cultural centres and clubs and larger clubs at the basic level have set up creative writing groups, literary review teams and amateur art troupes and hold exhibitions and theatrical festivals at regular intervals. Some of the cultural centres have organized workers' literary, art, calligraphic and photographic societies or associations. There are close on 30 literary journals published by trade unions or workers' cultural centres throughout the country. The following table shows the rapid expansion of workers' amateur writing groups and art troupes in 1980. 3) Promotion of recreational and sports

	Amateur art troupes		Amateur creative writing groups	
	Number of troupes	Number of participants	Number of groups	Number of participants
Total	15,715	330,537	8,883	53,396
Those run by basic-level units	14,015	294,741	8,279	45,906
Those run by units above the basic level	1,705	35,796	604	7,490

activities, such as chess, poker, stamp-collecting, gardening, bird raising, "lantern riddles" (a kind of guessing

game), entertainments and radio, and organization of
sports teams and matches. 4) Libraries (see Section One
for details). 5) Films. There are altogether 30,000 film-
projection units in trade unions at all levels, of which
10,000 have 35-mm projectors, or five times the number
of cinemas run by government cultural departments.

The management of workers' cultural centres and clubs
Management committees are elected by general meetings
of worker activists in their areas and comprise both full-
time staff and activists in mass cultural work.

Cultural centres and clubs obtain their funds from
three sources: allocations from trade unions at the next
higher levels, financial aid from government departments,
and proceeds from the programmes themselves. Clubs
are non-profit organizations. They give favoured treat-
ment to trade union members and their proceeds are used
entirely to support themselves.

Cultural centres and clubs in their activities adhere to
the principles of voluntary spare-time participation,
varied and small-scale activities, and economical and prac-
tical management. With the permission of their leaders,
workers and staff can take time off during work hours to
participate in theatrical festivals, athletic matches or
meetings, without loss of regular wages or bonuses.

4. CHILDREN'S CENTRES AND CLUBS

Children's centres and clubs are extracurricular educational establishments run by Communist Youth League
organizations and government educational departments.
They are also part of mass cultural work. Through sponsoring recreational and sports activities tailored to

children's needs, they co-operate with schools in developing communist spirit and moral character, widening knowledge, enriching cultural life, developing many-sided interests and abilities, and giving technological training. There are now children's centres and clubs in most cities, children's clubs in city districts and counties, and children's activity halls in basic-level units. According to statistics of 1981, there were 144 children's centres, 58 youths' centres, 596 children's clubs, 26 children's science and technology centres, and 7,130 children's activity halls throughout the country.

Children's centres and clubs sponsor mainly mass activities in culture, art and literature, science and technology, and sports. 1) Most of the children's centres and clubs have libraries, exhibition halls, recreational and slide show rooms, and some of the larger ones have cinemas, theatres, or sports grounds open to teenagers in their areas. 2) There are permanent groups for art and literature, science and technology, and sports, each with special instructors. These cover a wide range, such as playing musical instruments, singing, painting, dancing, embroidery, drama, puppetry, photography, poetry recitals, calligraphy, model aeroplane and ship building, radio reception and transmission, handiwork, carpentry, gardening, pets, physics, chemistry, mathematics, astronomy, meteorology, geology, ball games, gymnastics and traditional martial arts. There are full-time and part-time instructors, the latter being mostly engineers, scientists and experienced teachers devoted to children's welfare. The Shanghai Children's Centre run by the China Welfare Institute, for instance, has 82 specialists as part-time instructors. Members of the groups are recommended by their schools and admitted by examinations. Since its inauguration in 1956, the children's centre in Xicheng District in Beijing has run 76 groups in 27 activities, with a total of 4,000 members. The Taiyuan City Children's Centre has 35 regular groups with 500 members. While offering a wide choice of programmes to children, these groups also help train core members for extracurricular activities in schools and discover and recommend talented children for professional training. The children's centre in Hexi District in Tianjin, for instance, has recommended more than 40 talented children to professional art troupes and colleges in the past two years. 3) The children's centres and clubs often organize week-end parties, riddle-guessing evenings, story-telling, theatrical performances, athletic matches, art exhibitions, meetings with famous scientists and artists, and visits to factories and rural communes. 4) The children's centres and clubs also hold classes in literature, sports, science and technology to help train activists to assist in the work of the basic-level activity halls and extracurricular activities in schools.

Children's centres, clubs and activity halls are financed by the government out of its educational allocations, along with aid in facilities and equipment donated by factories and schools.

Chapter Three

MUSEUMS AND ARCHAEOLOGY

1. ARCHAEOLOGICAL AFFAIRS IN NEW CHINA

The establishment of archaeological institutions and regulations for the protection of artifacts and sites With one of the earliest civilizations in the world, China has a wealth of archaeological artifacts both above and under the ground. In the hundred years or so before the founding of the People's Republic, great damage was done to China's valuable cultural legacy as a result of imperialist aggression and the misrule of reactionary governments. Many valuable objects were smuggled out of China, ancient tombs were robbed, and ancient buildings, grottoes, temples and other sites were vandalized or fell into disrepair from long years of neglect. Shortly after the birth of the People's Republic, therefore, the Central People's Government issued a decree banning the export of valuable artifacts and art objects. This was followed by a number of other decrees and directives, in which the protection of artifacts and art objects was explicitly listed as a standard item in cultural work. Special institutions were set up at central and local levels to take charge of this work. At the top is the State Museums and Archaeological Materials Bureau, which is responsible for the work on a national scale. The Institute of Archaeology in the Chinese Academy of Sciences is responsible for organizing field investigations, excavations and research, and coordinating relevant central departments in examining and approving the excavation plans of local archaeological institutions and giving them technical guidance. At the provincial, municipal or autonomous regional level are the archaeological committees. Wherever possible in the provinces, municipalities or autonomous regions, museums and archaeological teams have been set up to take charge of the investigation, collection and protection of artifacts, sites and art objects as well as field work and research in their own areas.

Capital construction began on a nationwide scale in 1953 when the nation embarked on its First Five-Year Plan for National Economic Development. In view of this, the Central People's Government Administration Council promulgated a Directive Concerning the Protection of Historical and Revolutionary Relics in Capital Construction. This set the stage for the overall protection and administration of artifacts, sites and art objects centred on archaeological investigation and excavation in coordination with the undertaking of the capital construction projects. In 1958, when the movement for cooperative farming was at its height, the State Council published a Circular on Protecting Cultural Artifacts, Sites and Art Objects in Agricultural Production and Construction, calling for a universal survey of artifacts, sites and art objects and the designation of historical monuments for protection. In 1961, in the light of the experience gained in the protection of artifacts, sites and art objects in the 11 years since the founding of the People's Republic, it promulgated the Temporary Regulations Concerning the Protection and Administration of Artifacts, Sites and Art Objects and the Directive on Further

Strengthening the Protection and Administration of Artifacts, Sites and Art Objects.

The maintenance and protection of historical monuments As well as issuing decrees on the protection of artifacts, sites and art objects against vandalization, the government also makes an annual allocation for their maintenance and scientific protection against the whims of nature.

In the early days of the People's Republic, investigations were made into the condition of the country's ancient buildings and statuary caves, and necessary work was done to preserve those in bad repair. Systematic work began in 1952 on the repair and maintenance of a number of important ancient buildings and statuary caves. The cliff faces into which the Mogao Caves at Dunhuang, Gansu, were dug were reinforced and the crevices on the walls repaired to prevent cave-ins. A gigantic project was also undertaken to guard against destruction of the Yungang Caves in Datong by the elements. Architectural treasures in Beijing, such as the former imperial palaces, the Temple of Heaven, Beihai Park, the Summer Palace, the Ming emperors' tombs and the Great Wall at Badaling have been repaired or refurbished many times.

Major repairs and restoration work based on scientific investigation were also carried out on major ancient buildings. In 1953, major repairs were made to the two Song Dynasty (960-1279) halls in the Longxing Temple in Zhengding, Hebei. Five years later, in 1958, the decayed beams and slanting columns were repaired, the later additions were pulled down, and the buildings were restored to their original condition.

With the progress of national economic development,

the preservation of ancient buildings and sites often came into conflict with the building of capital construction projects. For this reason, the People's Government adopted the principle of taking into consideration both the needs of capital construction and the preservation of historical monuments. Consequently, a number of historical monuments were removed intact to make way for planned projects. When a large reservoir was to be built nearby, the Yongle Palace (1271-1368), a Taoist monastery famous for its Yuan Dynasty murals in Yongji, Shanxi, had to be removed to Ruicheng 22 kilometres away. Planning for the removal began in 1956 with the approval of the State Council, and actual work started in 1959 and was basically completed in 1966. The four halls were rebuilt according to their original form and the murals were lifted from the original walls and put back in the new halls after reinforcement and restoration.

Scientific research on techniques of preserving archaeological finds has made definite progress in the past three decades or more.

General surveys of artifacts, sites and art objects In 1950, the Museums and Archaeological Materials Bureau organized many inspection groups for surveys in major areas. This was followed by general surveys conducted by the provinces, municipalities and autonomous regions. Within a period of five to six years, investigations were made into 36,231 historical monuments and ancient buildings.

In June 1951, the Museums and Archaeological Materials Bureau sent a group of specialists to Dunhuang in Gansu for a general survey of the Mogao Caves. In October of the same year, when the Bingling Temple Grottoes was discovered in Yongjing, Gansu, an inspection group was sent to conduct surveys, take photographs and compile indices. The group also published a report on the results of their surveys. After the Tiantishan Caves and the Sigoubei Cave Temple were discovered in 1952 and 1960 in Wuwei and Qingyang (both in Gansu), systematic investigations were conducted into the caves, cave temples and cliff inscriptions and niches first in northwest China then in Sichuan, Yunnan, Henan, Hebei, Shanxi, Shandong, Jiangsu, Zhejiang and Inner Mongolia.

Many architectural treasures were discovered in the general survey of ancient buildings. Han Dynasty palace buildings alone were discovered in six places. The main hall of the Nanchan Temple built in 782 during the Tang Dynasty was found in the Wutai Mountains in Shanxi, the earliest wooden structure so far discovered. A number of buildings dating back to the Five Dynasties (907-960), the Liao Dynasty (961-1125) and the Song Dynasty were discovered in Shanxi and Hebei. Before Liberation, the Pure Trinity Hall of the Xuanmiao Temple in Suzhou was believed to be the only remaining Song wooden building in the south. Since Liberation, many more wooden buildings of that period have been found in Zhejiang, Fujian, Guangdong and Sichuan.

Investigations have also been made into some ancient private homes. In 1952, more than 20 private homes and ancestral temples of the Ming Dynasty (1368-1644) were found in Xiexian, Anhui. Later, many more were found in Jixi and Xiuning in the same province as well as in Shanxi, Zhejiang, Fujian and Jiangxi. An investigation in 1980 in Jingdezhen, Jiangxi, brought to light 136 houses, temples and gates dating back to the Ming Dynasty as well as a whole street of the same period more than 80 metres long. These ancient buildings from different periods form a fairly systematic material history of ancient Chinese architecture.

Historical monuments designated as under state protection These are buildings or sites which are unmovable or which should not be moved, and fall into two categories. The first category consists of ancient monuments such as old buildings, cave temples, stone carvings, historical sites and tombs; the second consists of modern and contemporary monuments such as revolutionary sites and memorials. The important artifacts, sites and art objects discovered in the general surveys are classified according to value for protection at different levels of the major administrative divisions. The most valuable are designated by the State Council as major national treasures under state protection. At the next level, each of the provinces, municipalities and autonomous regions also has artifacts, sites and art objects under its protection. In 1961, the State Council published the first list of 180 major national treasures under state protection (see appendices), followed by the second list of 62 in 1982 (see appendices). Museums, memorial halls, research institutes, conservation and preservation institutions and other specialized organizations have been set up as centres of administration, preservation and research. Ninety-seven of the first list of 180 major national treasures have special organizations of this kind.

Each of these special administrative centres has the following responsibilities. 1) The specification of the object under protection. Not only is the safety of revolutionary monuments, ancient buildings and caves to be ensured but the original surroundings should also be preserved as much as is possible. In the planning for a new construction project, consideration must be given to preserving the atmosphere of nearby major national treasures. As well as marking off the above-ground surroundings of ancient sites and tombs for general protection, the areas underground with particularly important treasures should be designated as major areas for protection, in which building and other activities liable to interfere with the earth around them are forbidden. Plans for building in general protection areas must be submitted to the appropriate administrative centre for approval. 2) The erection of plaques specifying the name of the artifact, site or art object, its grade, the name of its administrative centre and the date of its designation as a major national treasure, and describing its history and artistic and scientific value. 3) The scientific recording and maintenance of the historical documents, written records, rubbings, photos and charts to assist in research, maintenance, repair and excavation. 4) The assignment of special personnel and the establishment of special organizations to be responsible for the protection of the artifact, site or art object.

With a view to better protecting cities of historical interest or revolutionary importance, the State Council published in 1982 the first list of 24 such cities. These are Beijing, Chengde, Datong, Nanjing, Suzhou, Yangzhou, Hangzhou, Shaoxing, Quanzhou, Jingdezhen, Qufu, Luoyang, Kaifeng, Jiangling, Changsha, Guangzhou, Guilin, Chengdu, Zunyi, Kunming, Dali, Lhasa, Xi'an and Yan'an.

Large-scale archaeological investigations and excavations Archaeological investigations and excavations in new China have been carried out under the impetus of national economic construction. In the early period of the People's Republic, underground sites, artifacts and

art objects were often discovered in the course of building
of factories and water conservancy projects. In its relevant decrees, therefore, the Central People's Government
made specific, clear-cut provisions for the ways and means
of protecting artifacts, sites and art objects. It called
upon archaeological departments to co-operate closely
with construction units, incorporate the protection of
found objects in the plans of building undertaken in rich
archaeological sites, and carry out archaeological surveys
and excavations on construction sites.

Archaeological surveys and excavations were carried
out in every region in China along with the full-scale
unfolding of economic construction. The archaeological
excavations undertaken entirely by the Chinese before
Liberation were limited almost entirely to the Huanghe
valley and a part of the lower Changjiang valley. Since
the birth of the People's Republic, archaeological institutions well-staffed with specialists and archaeologists have
been set up in the provinces, municipalities and autonomous regions as well as in special administrative regions,
and archaeological investigations and excavations have
been carried out in every part of China: in the Heilongjiang valley in the northeast, on the Xisha Islands in the
south, on the Tibetan Plateau in the west, and in the
grasslands and deserts in Inner Mongolia and Xinjiang.
In field work, instead of digging a few ditches or tombs
as in pre-Liberation days, excavations are usually made
over vast areas in order to get an overall picture of the
ruins or tomb sites. This is the case with the two villages
of the primitive clan commune at Banpo, Xi'an, and
Jiangchai, Lintong, as well as Chang'an (now Xi'an),
capital of the Han and Tang dynasties and Beijing, capital
during the Yuan Dynasty. In these places, vast areas were

excavated in order to gain a picture of the overall arrangement or details of a part. In tomb excavations, the usual practice is to excavate all or the greater part of them so as to find out the distribution pattern of the tombs. In the case of the neolithic tombs, for instance, more than 1,600 of them were dug at Liuwan in Ledu, Qinghai, and upwards of 800 at Beiyao in Luoyang.

In short, archaeological work has made great headway in the past three decades or more, and the valuable cultural heritage of China shines with a new lustre in the new epoch.

2. MUSEUMS

Museums in China cover a wide range of fields, chiefly the Chinese revolution, military affairs, ethnic minorities, history, topology, natural science, arts, medicine, and science and technology. This section deals with the museums or memorial halls which exhibit, study and preserve archaeological and historical artifacts.

The period since the founding of new China has witnessed a swift expansion of museums. By the end of 1980, there were 366 museums in China, of which 54 were above the provincial, municipal or autonomous regional level, 117 at the regional or provincially administered city level, and 195 at the county or city-administered district level. The following chart shows the expansion of museums since 1949:

The progress of excavation and acquisition by purchase or donation has greatly enriched the collections in the state museums and provided a solid material foundation for their exhibitions and research. Research on artifacts

	1949	1957	1965	1970	1975	1978	1979	1980
Number of museums	21	72	214	165	242	349	344	366

has become a special discipline of the museums and added to the study of Chinese history. Using their own collections as a basis, museums throughout the country have held many exhibitions, contributing greatly to the popularization of historical knowledge, the elevation of the people's scientific and cultural levels and the spread of dialectical historical materialism.

Museums and Memorial Halls in China

BEIJING

Museum of Chinese History*

Museum of the Chinese Revolution*
Palace Museum*
Lu Xun Museum*
Capital Museum
Xu Beihong Museum

TIANJIN
Tianjin Museum of Natural Sciences
Tianjin Museum of History
Tianjin Art Museum
Commemoration Hall of the Early Life of Premier Zhou
    Enlai in Tianjin
Tianjin Santiaoshi Historical Museum

---

* Museums at the state level.

HEBEI
Artifacts Bureau of the Hebei Provincial Museum
Zhangjiakou Regional Museum
Dingxian County Museum
Qing Emperors' Temporary Palace Museum at Chengde
Li Dazhao Memorial Hall, Leting
Panjiayu Commemoration Hall, Fengjun
Norman Bethune Memorial Hall, Tangxian
Ranzhang Tunnel Warfare Commemoration Hall, Qingyuan
Norman Bethune's Operation Room Exhibition Hall, Hejian

SHANXI
Shanxi Provincial Museum
Yuncheng Regional Museum
Datong City Museum
Changzhi City Museum
Linfen City Museum
Jishan County Museum
Yuncheng County Museum
Yongji County Museum
Wanrong County Museum
Taihang Eighth Route Army Commemoration Hall
Jiexiu County Museum
Xihetou Tunnel Warfare Museum
Norman Bethune Memorial Hall, Songyankou
Caijiaya Commemoration Hall, Xingxian

INNER MONGOLIA
Inner Mongolia Autonomous Regional Museum
Jiren League Museum

LIAONING
Liaoning Provincial Museum

Chaoyang Regional Museum
Shenyang Palace Museum
Lushun Historical Museum
Fushun City Museum
Jinzhou City Museum
Jinxian County Museum
Resist-U.S.-Aggression-and-Aid-Korea Movement Museum, Dandong

JILIN
Jilin Provincial Museum
Jilin Revolutionary Museum
Baicheng Regional Museum
Jilin City Museum
Yushu County Museum
Siping City Revolutionary Commemoration Hall
Fuyu County Exhibition Hall
Da'an County Exhibition Hall
Yanbian Korean Autonomous Prefectural Museum
Changchun Revolutionary Martyrs Exhibition Hall
General Yang Jingyu Memorial Hall, Jingyu

HEILONGJIANG
Heilongjiang Provincial Museum
Northeast China Revolutionary Martyrs Memorial Hall
Liu Yingjun Exhibition Hall, Jiamusi
Aihui County Anti-Revisionism Exhibition Hall

SHANGHAI
Shanghai Museum
Lu Xun Memorial Hall
Zou Taofen Memorial Hall

Songjiang County Museum
Jiading County Museum

Qingpu County Museum
Commemoration Hall at the Site of the First National
    Congress of the Chinese Communist Party

JIANGSU
Nanjing Museum
Nanjing City Museum
Nanjing Museum of the History of the Taiping Heavenly
    Kingdom
Chinese Communist Party Delegation Commemoration
    Hall, the New Plum Garden Village, Nanjing
Wuxi City Museum
Xuzhou Museum
Changzhou City Museum
Suzhou Museum
Nantong Museum
Lianyungang City Museum
Qingjiang City Museum
Yancheng County Museum
Administration Office of Premier Zhou Enlai's Home,
    Huaian
New Fourth Army Headquarters Site Administration
    Office, Yancheng
Yangzhou Museum
Taizhou City Museum
Zhenjiang City Museum
Maoshan New Fourth Army Site Administration Office,
    Zhenjiang
Administration Office of the New Fourth Army's Eastern
    March Commemoration Hall, Huangqiao

ZHEJIANG
Zhejiang Provincial Museum
Jiaxing County Museum

Jiashan County Museum
Pinghu County Museum
Haining County Museum
Haiyan County Museum
Tongxiang County Museum
Deqing County Museum
Wuxing County Museum
Anji County Museum
Changxing County Museum
Linhai County Museum
Lu Xun Memorial Hall, Shaoxing
Pinghu Landlords' Manor Exhibition Hall
Nanhu Revolutionary Commemoration Hall, Jiaxing
Jiangsu-Zhejiang New Fourth Army Headquarters Site,
   Changxing
Yijiangshan Island Liberation Commemoration Hall

ANHUI
Anhui Provincial Museum
Bengfu City Museum
Huainan City Museum
Huaibei City Museum
Anqing City Museum
Huizhou Regional Museum
Fuyang Regional Museum
Haoxian County Museum
Xiaoxian County Museum
Shouxian County Museum
Xiexian County Museum
Jingxian County Museum

FUJIAN
Fujian Provincial Museum
Gutian Commemoration Hall

Museum of the History of Quanzhou's Sea Communications with Other Countries
Zhangzhou Commemoration Hall
Zheng Chenggong Memorial Hall, Xiamen
Changting Revolutionary Commemoration Hall
Ninghua County Revolutionary Commemoration Hall
Shanghang Revolutionary Commemoration Hall
Jianning County Revolutionary Commemoration Hall
Longyan Revolutionary Commemoration Hall
Caixi Township Investigation Commemoration Hall
Yongding Revolutionary Commemoration Hall
Xinquan Commemoration Hall
Lin Zexu Memorial Hall

JIANGXI
Jiangxi Provincial Revolutionary Museum
Jiangxi Provincial Museum of History
Nanchang "August the First" Uprising Commemoration Hall
Anyuan Railway and Mining Workers' Movement Commemoration Hall
Ruijin Revolutionary Commemoration Hall
Jinggangshan Revolutionary Museum
Bada Shanren Calligraphy and Painting Exhibition Hall
Nanchang County Historical Relics Exhibition Hall
Pingxiang City Museum
Lushan Museum
Ganzhou City Museum
Jingdezhen Ceramics Museum
Xunwu County Revolutionary History Commemoration Hall
Ningdu County Revolutionary History Commemoration Hall

Xingguo County Revolutionary History Commemoration Hall

Guangchang County Revolutionary History Commemoration Hall

Yudu County Revolutionary History Commemoration Hall

Anyuan County Revolutionary History Commemoration Hall

Huichang County Revolutionary History Commemoration Hall

Xinfeng County Three-Year Guerrilla War Exhibition Hall

Nankang County Historical Relics Exhibition Hall

Wuyuan County Museum

Leping County Cultural Relics Exhibition Hall

Qingjiang County Museum

Guixi County Cultural Relics Exhibition Hall

Fengcheng County Historical Relics Exhibition Hall

Yichun County Revolutionary Museum

Tonggu County Autumn Uprising Commemoration Hall

Luofang Conference Site Exhibition Hall, Xinyu

Shanggao County Revolutionary History Commemoration Hall

Gaoan County Revolutionary History Commemoration Hall

Huangmao Exhibition Hall, Wanzai

Linchuan County Cultural Relics Exhibition Hall

Le'an County Revolutionary History Commemoration Hall

Kangdu Conference Exhibition Hall, Nanfeng

Jiujiang City Museum

Ji'an City Revolutionary Commemoration Hall

Baiyunshan Battle Exhibition Hall, Taihe

Yongfeng County Revolutionary History Commemoration Hall

Jishui Investigation Exhibition Hall, Jishui

Hunan-Jiangxi Revolutionary Commemoration Hall, Yongxin

Ninggang County Revolutionary History Commemoration Hall

Suichuan County Revolutionary History Commemoration Hall

Xiajiang Conference Exhibition Hall, Xiajiang

Make-Revolution-by-One-Rifle Exhibition Hall, Lianhua

"February the Seventh" Conference Commemoration Hall, Ji'an

Jifeng Commemoration Hall, Xingan

Xingan County Historical Exhibition Hall

Suichuan County Historical Exhibition Hall

Jiujiang County Museum Preparatory Office

De'an County Historical Exhibition Hall

Xiushui County Historical Exhibition Hall

Xiushui County Autumn Harvest Uprising Commemoration Hall

SHANDONG

Shandong Provincial Museum

Ji'nan City Museum

Qingdao City Museum

Qingdao Marine Products Museum

Zibo City Museum

Weifang City Museum

Yidu County Museum

Zhucheng County Museum

Liaocheng Regional Museum

Yantai City Museum

HENAN
Henan Provincial Museum
Zhengzhou City Museum
Kaifeng City Museum
Luoyang City Museum
Anyang City Museum
Hebi City Museum
Xinxiang City Museum
Jiaozuo City Museum
Nanyang City Museum
Junxian County Museum
Zhugou Commemoration Hall, Queshan

HUBEI
Hubei Provincial Museum
Longzhong Commemoration Hall, Xiangfan
Huangshi City Museum
Eighth Route Army Office
Wuchang Peasant Movement Institute
"August the Seventh" Conference Site
Jingzhou Regional Museum
Xiangyang Regional Museum
Huanggang Regional Museum
Suixian County Museum
Honghu County Revolutionary Museum
Xishui County Museum
Hongan County Revolutionary Museum
Echeng County Museum
Dawu County Revolutionary Museum
Yangxin County Revolutionary Museum
Macheng County Revolutionary Museum
Qu Yuan Temple Memorial Hall, Zigui
Xuanhuadian Commemoration Hall, Dawu
Longgang Commemoration Hall, Yangxin

Qiliping Commemoration Hall, Hongan
Qujiawan Commemoration Hall, Honghu

HUNAN

Western Hunan Tujia-Miao Autonomous Prefectural
  Museum
Hunan Provincial Museum
Hengyang City Museum
Chairman Mao Zedong's Home Exhibition Hall, Shaoshan
Exhibition Hall at the Site of the Hunan Regional Com-
  mittee of the Chinese Communist Party
Changsha First Normal School Exhibition Hall
Hunan Independent Study University
Wangluyuan Exhibition Hall
Xiangxiang County Museum
Hunan Students' Union Exhibition Hall
Autumn Uprising Exhibition Hall at the Wenjiashi Site
Guidong County Exhibition Hall
Temple of King Kang Exhibition Hall, Hengshan
Lingxian County Exhibition Hall
Xiannongtan Exhibition Hall, Liling
Leifeng Memorial Hall
Yang Kaihui's Home Commemoration Hall
Ouyang Hai Memorial Hall
Ren Bishi Memorial Hall
Dongshan School Exhibition Hall, Xiangxiang

GUANGDONG

Guangdong Provincial Museum
Lu Xun Memorial Hall
Zhanjiang Regional Museum
Guangzhou City Museum
Guangzhou Peasant Movement Institute Site Com-
  memoration Hall

Guangdong Revolutionary History Museum
Guangdong Folk Arts Hall
Guangzhou Art Gallery
Site of the Guangdong Regional Committee of the Chinese
    Communist Party
Sanyuanli People's Anti-British Struggle Commemoration
    Hall
Huanghuagang Uprising Headquarters Site
Vietnamese Youth Training Class Site
Guangzhou Uprising Commemoration Hall
Wugong Temple at Haikou City
Shantou City Museum
Zumiao Temple, Foshan
Ye Ting's Independent Regiment Site, Zhaoqing
Meizhou City Museum
Chaoan County Museum
Chenghai County Museum
Jieyang County Museum
Puning County Museum
Red Palace and Square, Haifeng
Dapu County Museum
Sun Yat-sen's Home Commemoration Hall
Xinhui County Museum
Zijin County Museum
Dongwan County Museum
Hong Xiuquan's Home Commemoration Hall
Humen Anti-British Struggle Commemoration Hall,
    Dongwan

GUANGXI
Guangxi Zhuang Autonomous Regional Museum
Wuzhou City Museum
Liuzhou City Museum

Youjiang Revolutionary History Hall
Donglan Revolutionary Commemoration Hall
Hepu County Museum
Youjiang Revolutionary Commemoration Hall, Tiandong

SICHUAN
Sichuan Provincial Museum
Chongqing City Museum
Liangshan Yi Autonomous Prefectural Museum
U.S.-Chiang Kai-shek Criminal Activities Exhibition
   Hall, Chongqing
Zigong City Salt Manufacture History Museum
Dayi County Landlords' Manor Exhibition Hall
Garze Tibetan Autonomous Prefectural Exhibition Hall
Hongyan Revolutionary Commemoration Hall, Chongqing
Du Fu's Thatched Hut Memorial Hall, Chengdu
Qiu Shaoyun Memorial Hall, Tongliang
Li Bai Memorial Hall, Jiangyou
Zhao Yiman Memorial Hall, Yibin
Zhang Side Exhibition Hall
Huang Jiguang Memorial Hall, Zhongjiang
Comrade Zhu De Exhibition Hall, Yilong
Sichuan-Shaanxi Revolutionary Base Museum

GUIZHOU
Guizhou Provincial Museum
Zunyi Conference Commemoration Hall

YUNNAN
Yunnan Provincial Museum
Zha Xi Memorial Hall, Zhaotong
Kedu Exhibition Hall, Qujing

SHAANXI
Shaanxi Provincial Museum
Banpo Museum, Xi'an

Museum of Qin Shi Huang's Buried Legion Sculpture
The Eighth Route Army Office Commemoration Hall,
  Xi'an
Chezhanggou Class Education Hall, Xi'an
Machang Landlord Crimes Exhibition Hall, Chang'an
Yaozhou Kiln Museum, Tongchuan
Xianyang City Museum
Du Fu Memorial Hall, Chang'an
Bailiang Village Class Education Hall, Xianyang
Mengdian Class Education Hall, Sanyuan
Qianling Mausoleum Museum
Maoling Mausoleum Museum, Xingping
Zhaoling Mausoleum Museum, Liquan
Baoji City Museum
Tangjia Class Education Hall, Xunyi
Longxian County Class Education Hall
Fengxiang County Class Education Hall
Hanzhong County Museum
Fufeng County Class Education Hall
Yangxian County Class Education Hall
Yan'an Revolutionary Commemoration Hall
Luochuan Conference Site
Suide County Museum

GANSU
Gansu Provincial Museum
Qingyang Regional Museum
Linxia Hui Autonomous Prefectural Museum
Wuwei Regional Museum
Qingyang County Museum
Jiuquan County Museum

QINGHAI
Qinghai Provincial Museum Preparatory Office

NINGXIA

Ningxia Hui Autonomous Regional Museum

XINJIANG

Xinjiang Uygur Autonomous Regional Museum

The Museum of Chinese History was founded in 1959. Its origins go back to the Museum of History established in July 1912, which became Beijing Museum of History after Liberation in 1949. In 1959 the museum was moved to its present site on the east side of Tiananmen Square and made into a national historical museum.

The Museum of Chinese History is a socialist state museum of a new type devoted to the general history of China. Its responsibilities are to collect and preserve materials from ancient and modern Chinese history, hold exhibitions and carry out scientific research. It has more than 300,000 items, mainly dating from pre-Liberation times, such as bronze wares, coins, ceramics, silk fabrics, calligraphy, paintings, rubbings from stone tablets and bronze vessels, and documents. Its collection also includes more than 200,000 Chinese books, several hundred Chinese journals and more than 2,000 foreign publications. Many of the objects and publications are extremely rare or even the only ones still in existence.

The Exhibition of General Chinese History is a permanent exhibition, which opened to the public in July 1961 after a 21-month preview. Covering a floor space of more than 8,000 square metres, the display includes more than 9,000 valuable historical relics, ranging from the time of the primitive man of one million years ago to the May 4 Movement of 1919. It is divided into four major parts representing the stages of Chinese social development — primitive, slave, feudal and semi-colonial,

semi-feudal (the old-democratic revolution period) societies. The exhibition highlights the fine revolutionary
traditions of the Chinese people, and also presents in a
systematic and scientific way the long history of the
Chinese nation in terms of class struggle, the struggle for
production, scientific and cultural development, external
contacts and the formation of a united, multi-ethnic
country.

The Museum of Chinese Revolution Formally inaugurated in 1960. A Central Revolutionary Museum Preparatory Office was first established in 1953, and moved
to the present site of the museum on the east side of
Tiananmen Square in 1959.

The Museum of Chinese Revolution is another socialist
state museum of a new type, which is responsible for the
collection and preservation of revolutionary artifacts,
photographs and other materials, the presentation of exhibitions on the history of the Chinese Communist Party
and modern Chinese history, and conducting scientific
research. It has a collection of almost 100,000 items,
mainly dating from after the May 4 Movement of 1919,
such as proclamations, documents, inscriptions by famous
revolutionaries and others, manuscripts and photographs.
Its collection also includes about 5,000 rare publications.

The Exhibition of the History of the Chinese Communist
Party, the permanent exhibition of the museum, opened
on July 1, 1961. Covering a floor space of 4,000 square
metres, it displays more than 3,300 items representing the
history of the new-democratic revolution and the history
of the socialist revolution and construction led by the
Chinese Communist Party since the May 4 Movement.

The Palace Museum One of the largest and oldest
state museums in China, it specializes in preserving the

imperial palaces and palace objects of the Ming (1368-1644) and Qing (1644-1911) dynasties along with other traditional arts and crafts, and is also responsible for their study and exhibition. A part of the imperial palaces was first opened as a museum in 1914, when a permanent Exhibition of Antiques was held there. During the rule of the Kuomintang, many of the palace treasures were stolen and the buildings fell into disrepair. After the liberation of Beijing in 1949, the Palace Museum was taken over by the People's Government and put directly under the administration of the State Museums and Archaeological Materials Bureau.

The Palace Museum has more than 900,000 items from the palace treasures and other traditional arts and crafts, including calligraphy, paintings, ceramics, bronze vessels, stone tablets and embroideries. Many of them are unique to this collection.

Two permanent exhibitions in the Palace Museum are the Exhibition of Palace History of the Ming and Qing and the Traditional Arts and Crafts Exhibition. The Exhibition of Palace History covers more than 6,000 square metres in 17 halls and has on display more than 2,400 exhibits. The exhibition illustrates the grand ceremonies held by the Qing emperors, the daily activities of the government and the living conditions of the emperors and empresses. The Traditional Arts and Crafts Exhibition consists of five halls with a total floor space of more than 4,000 square metres. It contains almost 3,000 exhibits such as paintings, ceramics, bronzes, jewels and precious stones, and Ming and Qing arts and crafts. The exhibitions of clocks and watches and the arts of many dynasties are in preparation.

The Museum of Qin Shi Huang's Buried Legion Sculp-

ture   The largest display of ancient military arts in China, this museum is built over the three underground vaults excavated on the east side of the mausoleum of Emperor Qin Shi Huang of the Qin Dynasty (r. 246-210 B.C.) on the northern foothills of Lishan Mountain in Lintong, Shaanxi. Each of the three vaults contains life-size figures of warriors and chariots. Vault One was discovered when local peasants were sinking wells to fight a drought in 1974. It is in the form of a tunnel built of earth and timber, 230 metres long, 62 metres wide and 5 metres high, and is filled with a large number of life-size terra-cotta warriors and horses in battle formation. Some of the charioteers are as high as 1.92 metres. Three rows of soldiers in brown armour and with bows and arrows stand facing east, forming the vanguard. Behind them is the main body of the army, thousands of armour-clad soldiers in 38 columns around the chariots. They also face east and are armed with spears and dagger-axes. There are also flank and rear guards, each in a separate file, which stand with their backs to the chariots, guarding against enemy interception and encirclement. Altogether 10,000 real weapons have been unearthed, all cast of an alloy of copper and tin coated with rustproof chromium, as well as poisonous arrow-heads, also cast of an alloy of copper and lead, which still remain sharp today. The terra-cotta figures are true to life, each with different features and expressions; together they form a miniature Qin army and provide valuable materials for the study of the military affairs, politics, economy, culture and arts of the Qin Dynasty. The main exhibition hall of the museum, which is built over Vault One, was opened to the public on October 1, 1979.

3. EXHIBITIONS OF CHINESE ARCHAEOLOGICAL FINDS ABROAD

With a view to promoting friendly relations and cultural exchanges with other countries, China has held exhibitions of its archaeological finds in more than ten countries. These exhibitions have been well-received by people abroad.

Between the 1950s and 1960s, China held a number of exhibitions in the Soviet Union, Poland, Czechoslovakia and Japan. These included exhibitions of Dunhuang murals (reproductions), the Yongle Palace murals (reproductions), ancient ceramics, rubbings from Xi'an stone tablets, and old editions of the famous traditional Chinese novel *A Dream of Red Mansions*. From May 1973 to April 1978, exhibitions were also held in France, Japan, Britain, Romania, Austria, Yugoslavia, Sweden, Mexico, Canada, Holland, the United States, Belgium, the Philippines, Australia, and Hong Kong. These included six archaeological finds exhibitions as well as exhibitions of slab paintings and stone tablet rubbings from Henan, Han and Tang murals, Ming and Qing arts and crafts, and ancient bronzes. The exhibits were chosen from the large selections of artifacts excavated from all parts of China in the previous two decades or more, ranging in time from the primitive society of the New Stone Age to the Ming Dynasty and providing a general outline of traditional Chinese culture. Exhibitions of Chinese archaeological finds have been regarded as important cultural events in the countries in which they were held. In his speech at the opening ceremony of a Chinese exhibition in the Philippines, President Marcos said that the Chinese archaeological finds exhibition was a great cultural event both Beijing and Manila should be proud of. Wherever they were held, these exhibitions were given extensive coverage by the local press, broadcasting and television stations. The Public Broadcasting Service and the Columbia Broadcasting System in the United States each made a film lasting over an hour on the Chinese archaeological exhibition, which was broadcast several times. The Chinese exhibitions have also drawn large crowds. The one held in London was visited by 770,000 people in four months, outnumbering all previous attendances at art exhibitions held there.

In 1980, the Chinese Archaeological Finds Exhibition Working Committee held a number of exhibitions in the United States, Britain, Denmark, Switzerland, West Germany and Belgium. The Great Chinese Bronze Age Exhibition, the largest of its kind ever held in the United States, had on display almost 100 bronze wares selected from among the many finds of the previous three decades by the museums and archaeological units of Hebei, Henan, Shaanxi and 12 other provinces and municipalities. The exhibits dated from the Erlitou Culture of the legendary Xia Dynasty around the 21st century B.C. to the Han Dynasty. U.S. museum officials considered the exhibition the most sensational event in that country in 1980.

The Exhibition of Chinese Jewels and Precious Stones, part of the cultural exchange programmes between China and Denmark, Switzerland, West Germany and Belgium, opened in May 1980 in Denmark and closed in Belgium in May the following year. The exhibition was well received in each country. It displayed a rich assortment of treasures ranging from the painted pottery vessels 6,000 years old to the glittering gold ware of the Tang Dynasty.

The Exhibition of Ancient Chinese Ceramic Kiln Sites, an academic exhibition held in Britain at the invitation of the British Museum and the Ashmolean Museum in Oxford, displayed mainly broken porcelain shards unearthed from the kiln sites dating from the Han to the Yuan dynasties. Ceramic specialists in Britain and other countries welcomed the exhibition and were impressed by its display.

Appendices

The First Selection of Historical Monuments Designated for State Protection

(1) Revolutionary Sites and Memorial Buildings (33)

Name	Period	Location	Remarks
Quell-the-British Corps Site	1841	Sanyuanli, Guangzhou	
Jintian Uprising Site	1851	Jintian Village, Guiping Guangxi	
Residence of Prince Zhong of the Taiping Heavenly Kingdom	1860	Suzhou, Jiangsu	
Chairman Mao Zedong's Home	1893	Shaoshan Village, Xiangtan, Hunan	
Zongshan Anti-British Struggle Site	1904	Gyangze, Tibet	
Tomb of the Seventy-two Martyrs at Huanghuagang	1911	Guangzhou	
Wuchang Uprising Military Government Site	1911	Wuhan City	

Name	Period	Location	Remarks
The Red Hall of Beijing University	1860	Shatan, Dongcheng District, Beijing	In commemoration of the May 4 Movement
Sun Yat-sen's Home	1919	Xiangshan Road, Shanghai	
Chinese Socialist Youth League Central Office Site	1920-21	Yuyangli, Huaihai Road, Shanghai	
Site of First National Congress of Chinese Communist Party	1921	Xingye Road, Shanghai	
Peasant Movement Institute Site	1926	4th Zhongshan Road, Guangzhou	
"August First" Uprising Headquarters Site	1927	Nanchang	
Site at Wenjiashi, where two insurgent units of the Autumn Uprising joined forces	1927	Liuyang, Hunan	
Red Palace and Square Site	1927-28	West Zhongshan Road, Haifeng County, Guangdong	

Name	Period	Location	Remarks
Guangzhou Commune Site	1927	Weixin Road, Guangzhou	
Jinggang Mountains Revolutionary Site	1927-29	Ninggang, Jiangxi	
Gutian Conference Site	1929	Gutian Village, Shanghang, Fujian	
Sun Yat-sen Mausoleum	1929	Purple Hill, Nanjing	
Ruijin Revolutionary Site	1931-34	Ruijin, Jiangxi	
Zunyi Conference Site	1935	Zunyi, Guizhou	
Luding Bridge		Luding, Garze, Sichuan	In commemoration of the Red Army's fight for the control of the iron chain bridge on its Long March in 1935
Yan'an Revolutionary Site	1937-47	Yan'an, Shaanxi	
Lugouqiao		Fengtai District, Beijing	Site includes the old county town of Wanping. In commemoration of the nationwide War of Resistance Against Japan that broke out on July 7, 1937

Name	Period	Location	Remarks
Pingxingguan Battle Site	1937	Fanzhi and Lingqiu, Shanxi	
Eighth Route Army Headquarters	1938	Wuxiang, Shanxi	
New Fourth Army Headquarters	1938-41	Jingxian, Anhui	
Eighth Route Army Office	1938-46	Hongyan Village, and Zengjiayan, Chongqing	
Ranzhuang Tunnel Warfare Site	1942	Baoding, Hebei	
Tiananmen Gatetower		Beijing	Site of the inauguration of the People's Republic of China in 1949. First built in the Ming Dynasty and rebuilt and refurbished many times since
Tomb of Lu Xun		Hongkou Park, Shanghai	Moved there in 1956
Sino-Soviet Friendship Monument	1957	Luda	
Monument to the People's Heroes	1958	Tiananmen Square, Beijing	

(2) Cave Temples (14)

Name	Period	Location	Remarks
Yungang Caves	Northern Wei	Datong, Shanxi	
Mogao Caves	Northern Wei to Yuan	Dunhuang, Gansu	Includes West Thousand-Buddha Caves
Yulin Caves	Northern Wei to Yuan	Anxi, Gansu	
Longmen Caves	Northern Wei to Tang	Luoyang, Henan	Includes the Tomb of Bai Juyi
Maijishan Caves	Northern Wei to Ming	Tianshui, Gansu	
Bingling Temple Caves	Northern Wei to Ming	Linxia, Gansu	
Xiangtangshan Caves	Eastern Wei, Northern Qi to Yuan	Handan, Hebei	
Gizr Thousand-Buddha Cave	Tang to Song	Baicheng, Xinjiang	Said to have been cut in the 3rd century

Name	Period	Location	Remarks
Kummitula Thousand-Buddha Cave	Tang to Song	Kuqa, Xinjiang	Said to have been cut in the 3rd century
Huangze Temple Cliff Sculptures	Tang	Guangyuan, Sichuan	
Thousand-Buddha Cliff Sculptures	Tang to Song	Guangyuan, Sichuan	
Beishan Cliff Sculptures	Tang to Song	Dazu, Sichuan	Includes Fowan, Guanyinpo, Foerfeng and Yingpanshan
Baodingshan Cliff Sculptures	Song	Dazu, Sichuan	Includes Dafowan, Xiaofowan, Guangdashan, Longtan and Linsongpo
Shizhongshan Caves	Kingdoms of Nanzhao and Dali (649-1094)	Jianchuan, Dali, Yunnan	Includes Shizhongsi, Shiziguan and Shadeng

(3) Ancient Buildings and Memorials (77)

Name	Period	Location	Remarks
Taishi Tower	Eastern Han	Dengfeng, Henan	
Shaoshi Tower	Eastern Han	Dengfeng, Henan	
Qimu Tower	Eastern Han	Dengfeng, Henan	
Feng Huan Tower	Eastern Han	Quxian, Sichuan	
Pingyang Prefect's Tower	Eastern Han	Mianyang, Sichuan	
Prefect Shen's Tower	Eastern Han	Quxian, Sichuan	
Stone Memorial Hall at Guo's Tomb on Xiaotang Mountain	Eastern Han	Feicheng, Shandong	
Stone Carvings at Tombs of Wu Family at Jiaxiang	Eastern Han	Jining, Shandong	
Tower and Stone Carvings at Gao Yi's Tomb	Eastern Han	Ya'an, Sichuan	
Baoxiedao Stone Gate and Cliff Inscriptions	Han to Song	Hanzhong City, Shaanxi	

Name	Period	Location	Remarks
Anji (Greater Stone) Bridge	Sui	Ningjin, Hebei	
Anping (Wuli) Bridge	Southern Song	Jinjiang, Fujian	
Yongtong (Lesser Stone) Bridge	Jin	Ningjin, Hebei	
Songyue Temple Pagoda	Northern Wei	Dengfeng, Henan	
Simen Pagoda	Eastern Wei	Licheng, Shandong	
Greater Wild Geese Pagoda	Tang	Xi'an, Shaanxi	
Lesser Wild Geese Pagoda	Tang	Xi'an, Shaanxi	
Three Pagodas at Chongsheng Temple	Tang and Five Dynasties	Dali, Yunnan	
Yunju Temple Pagoda and Stone Sutra	Sui, Tang, Liao, Jin	Fangshan, Beijing	
Xingjiao Temple Pagoda	Tang	Chang'an, Shaanxi	Includes the Xingjiao Temple and annexes
Yunyan Temple Pagoda	Five Dynasties	Suzhou, Jiangsu	Includes Yunyan Temple and annexes
Yuguo Temple Iron Pagoda	Northern Song	Kaifeng, Henan	

Name	Period	Location	Remarks
Kaiyuan Temple Pagoda	Northern Song	Dingxian, Hebei	
Sakyamuni Wooden Pagoda at Fogong Temple	Liao	Yingxian, Shanxi	
Six Harmonies Pagoda	Southern Song	Hangzhou, Zhejiang	
Hua Pagoda at Guanghui Temple	Jin	Zhengding, Hebei	
White Dagoba at Miaoying Temple	Yuan	Xicheng, Beijing	
Wuta Temple Pagoda	Ming	Haidian, Beijing	
Haibao Pagoda	Qing	Yinchuan, Ningxia	
Yicihui Stone Pillar	Northern Qi	Yixian, Hebei	
Dharani Scripture Pillars at Zhaozhou	Northern Song	Ningjin, Hebei	
Main Hall at Nanchan Temple	Tang	Wutai, Shanxi	
Foguang Temple	Tang to Qing	Wutai, Shanxi	

Name	Period	Location	Remarks
Juglakang (Jok-han) Monastery		Lhasa, Tibet	Built in the mid-7th century and re-built and refurbished many times
Changzhug Monastery		Nedong, Tibet	Said to have been built in the 7th century
Guangxiao Temple	Five Dynasties to Ming	Guangzhou	
Dule Temple	Liao	Jixian, Hebei	
Jinci Temple	Song	Taiyuan, Shanxi	
Fengguo Temple	Liao	Yixian, Liaoning	
Qingjing Temple	Song	Quanzhou, Fujian	
Shanhua Temple	Liao, Jin	Datong, Shanxi	
Longxing Temple	Song	Zhengding, Hebei	
Baoguo Temple	Northern Song	Yuyao, Zhejiang	
Huayan Temple	Liao, Jin, Qing	Datong, Shanxi	
White Horse Temple	Jin to Qing	Luoyang, Henan	Built on the site of the temple of the Eastern Han Dynasty

Name	Period	Location	Remarks
Yongle Palace	Yuan	Ruicheng, Shanxi	
Golden Hall on Wudang Mountain	Yuan, Ming	Guanghua, Hubei	
Sagya Monastery	Yuan	Sagya, Tibet	
Guangsheng Temple	Yuan, Ming	Hongdong, Shanxi	
Observatory	Yuan	Dengfeng, Henan	
Cloud Terrace at Juyongguan	Yuan	Changping, Beijing	
Confucian Temple and House	Jin to Qing	Qufu, Shandong	
Imperial Palace (Forbidden City)	Ming, Qing	Beijing	
Great Wall at Badaling	Ming	Yanqing, Beijing	
Great Wall at Shanhaiguan	Ming	Qinhuang-dao, Hebei	
Great Wall at Jiayuguan	Ming	Jiuquan, Gansu	
Xi'an City Wall	Ming	Xi'an, Shaanxi	

Name	Period	Location	Remarks
Temple of Heaven	Ming	Chongwen, Beijing	
Beihai Park and Round City	Ming, Qing	Xicheng, Beijing	
Potala Palace	Ming to the Republic of China	Lhasa, Tibet	
Ganden Monastery	Early Ming to Qing	Lhasa, Tibet	
Zhaxilhunbu Monastery	Early Ming to Qing	Xigaze, Tibet	
Zhihua Temple	Ming	Dongcheng, Beijing	
Taer Temple	Ming	Huang-zhong, Qinghai	
Imperial Palace	Qing	Shenyang, Liaoning	
Imperial College	Qing	Dongcheng, Beijing	
Yonghegong Lama Temple	Qing	Dongcheng, Beijing	
Puning Temple	Qing	Chengde, Hebei	
Pule Temple	Qing	Chengde, Hebei	

Name	Period	Location	Remarks
Temple of the Potaraka Doctrine	Qing	Chengde, Hebei	
Temple of Sumeru Happiness and Longevity	Qing	Chengde, Hebei	
Zhuge Liang Memorial Hall	Qing	Chengdu, Sichuan	
Du Fu Memorial Hall	Qing	Chengdu, Sichuan	
Humble Administrator's Garden	Ming, Qing	Suzhou, Jiangsu	
Summer Palace	Qing	Haidian, Beijing	
Imperial Summer Resort	Qing	Chengde, Hebei	
Linger-Here Garden	Qing	Suzhou, Jiangsu	

(4) Stone Carvings and Others (11)

Name	Period	Location	Remarks
Forest of Steles	Han to modern times	Xi'an, Shaanxi	

Name	Period	Location	Remarks
Cuan Baozi Stele	Eastern Jin	Qujing, Yunnan	
Cuan Longyan Stele	Southern Dynasties	Luliang, Yunnan	
Yaowangshan Stone Inscriptions	Sui to Ming	Tongchuan, Shaanxi	
Union Tablet of Duan Family with 37 Tribes	Kingdom of Dali (937-1094)	Qujing, Yunnan	
Tablet Marking Rebuilding of Ganying Pagoda at Huguo Temple	Xixia (1032-1227)	Wuwei, Gansu	
Stone Inscriptions at Confucian Temple	Southern Song	Suzhou, Jiangsu	
Xizhou Bronze Column	Five Dynasties	Yongshun, Hunan	

Name	Period	Location	Remarks
Bronze and Iron Buddha Images at Shengshou-wannian Temple, Emei Mountain	Song to Ming	Emei, Sichuan	
Iron Lion at Cangzhou	Later Zhou	Cangxian, Hebei	
Sculptures of Arhats at Bao-sheng Temple	Northern Song	Wuxian, Jiangsu	Once said to have been made by Yang Huizhi of the Tang

(5) Ancient Sites (26)

Name	Period	Location	Remarks
Zhoukoudian	Palaeolithic	Fangshan, Beijing	
Dingcun	Palaeolithic	Linfen, Shanxi	
Yangshao	Neolithic	Mianchi, Henan	
Banpo	Neolithic	Xi'an, Shaanxi	
Chengziya	Neolithic	Zhangqiu, Shandong	

Name	Period	Location	Remarks
Shang Site	Shang	Zhengzhou, Henan	
Yin Ruins	Yin	Anyang, Henan	
Feng and Gao, former capitals	Zhou	Chang'an, Shaanxi	
Linzi, former capital of Qi	Zhou	Yidu, Shandong	
Qufu, former capital of Lu	Zhou to Han	Qufu, Shandong	
Houma, Site of Jin	Eastern Zhou	Houma, Shanxi	
Jinan, former capital of Chu	Eastern Zhou	Jiangling, Hubei	
Zheng and Han, former capitals	Eastern Zhou	Xinzheng, Henan	
Handan, former capital of Zhao	Warring States	Handan, Hebei	
Secondary Capital of Yan	Warring States	Yixian, Hebei	
Epang Palace Site	Qin	Xi'an, Shaanxi	
Chang'an, former capital of Han Dynasty	Western Han	Xi'an, Shaanxi	

Name	Period	Location	Remarks
Luoyang, former capital of Han and Wei	Eastern Han to Northern Wei	Luoyang, Henan	
Gaochang, former capital	State of Gaochang (500–640)	Turpan, Xinjiang	
Yaerhu, former capital	State of Gaochang (500–640)	Turpan, Xinjiang	
Daming Palace	Tang	Xi'an, Shaanxi	
Taihe	State of Nanzhao (649–902)	Dali, Yunnan	Includes Dehua Tablet
Longquan, former capital of Bohai	State of Bohai (698–926)	Ningan, Heilongjiang	
Capital of Liao	Liao	Bairin Left Banner, Inner Mongolia	
Middle Capital of Liao	Liao	Ningcheng, Inner Mongolia	
Site of Guge Kingdom		Zanda, Tibet	

(6) Ancient Tombs (19)

Name	Period	Location	Remarks
Huangdi Mausoleum		Huangling, Shaanxi	
Tomb of Confucius	Eastern Zhou	Qufu, Shandong	
Qin Shi Huang Mausoleum	Qin	Lintong, Shaanxi	
Maoling Mausoleum	Western Han	Xingping, Shaanxi	Tomb of Emperor Wudi of the Han
Tomb of Huo Qubing	Western Han	Xingping, Shaanxi	
Tombs with murals	Han, Wei	Liaoyang, Liaoning	
Ancient tombs at Donggou	Korea (37 B.C.-A.D. 668)	Ji'an, Jilin	Includes Good King Tablet
Feng family tombs	Northern Wei to Sui	Wuqiao, Hebei	
Zhaoling Mausoleum	Tang	Qianxian, Shaanxi	Tomb of Emperor Taizong of the Tang
Qianling Mausoleum	Tang	Qianxian, Shaanxi	Tombs of Emperor Gaozong and Empress Wuzetian of the Tang

Name	Period	Location	Remarks
Shunling Mausoleum	Tang	Xianyang, Shaanxi	Tomb of Wuzetian's mother
Ancient tombs at Liudingshan	State of Bohai (698-926)	Dunhua, Yanbian, Jilin	
Royal Tibetan tombs	7th century	Qonggyai, Tibet	
Tomb of Wang Jian	Former Shu of the Five Dynasties	Chengdu, Sichuan	
Tomb of Yue Fei	Southern Song	Hangzhou, Zhejiang	
Xiaoling Mausoleum	Ming	Nanjing, Jiangsu	Tomb of Emperor Taizu of the Ming
Ming Tombs	Ming	Changping, Beijing	
East Imperial Tombs	Qing	Zunhua, Hebei	
West Imperial Tombs	Qing	Yixian, Hebei	

The Second Selection of Historical Monuments Designated for State Protection

(1) Revolutionary Sites and Memorial Buildings (10)

Name	Period	Location	Remarks
Site of Opium Burning and Humen Fortress	1839	Dongwan, Guangdong	
Residence of the Taiping Heavenly King	1853-64	Nanjing, Jiangsu	
Site of Yi He Tuan's Shrine to Lu Dongbin	1900	Tianjin	
Anyuan Railway and Mining Workers' Club	1922	Pingxiang, Jiangxi	
"August the Seventh" Conference Site	1927	Wuhan, Hubei	
Xi'an Incident Site	1936	Xi'an, Shaanxi	
Norman Bethune Model Hospital Ward	1938	Wutai, Shanxi	

Name	Period	Location	Remarks
Chinese Communist Party Central Committee Headquarters at Xibaipo	1948	Pingshan, Hebei	
Soong Ching Ling's Home	1963	Beiheyan, Beijing	
Tomb of Soong Ching Ling	1981	Wanguo Cemetery, Shanghai	

(2) Cave Temples (5)

Name	Period	Location	Remarks
Gongxian Caves	Northern Wei to Song	Gongxian, Henan	
Sumeru Hill Caves	Northern Dynasties to Tang	Guyuan, Ningxia	
Giant Buddha	Tang	Leshan, Sichuan	
Baizikelike Thousand-Buddha Cave	Tang to Yuan	Turpan, Xinjiang	
Feilaifeng Hill Sculptures	Five Dynasties to Yuan	Hangzhou, Zhejiang	

(3) Ancient Buildings and Memorials (28)

Name	Period	Location	Remarks
Xiuding Temple Pagoda	Tang	Anyang, Henan	
Jade Spring Temple and Iron Pagoda	Song	Dangyang, Hubei	
Ten-Thousand-Fascicle Avatamsaka-sutra Pagoda	Liao	Hohhot, Inner Mongolia	
Hualin Temple Main Hall	Song	Fuzhou, Fujian	
Kaiyuan Temple	Song to Qing	Quanzhou, Fujian	
Lingyan Temple	Tang to Qing	Changqing, Shandong	
Pure Trinity Hall at Xuanmiao Temple	Song	Suzhou, Jiangsu	
Yanshan Temple	Jin	Fanshi, Shanxi	
Beiyue Temple	Yuan	Quyang, Hebei	
Zixiao Palace	Ming	Junxian, Hubei	

Name	Period	Location	Remarks
Xiantong Temple	Ming to Qing	Wutai, Shanxi	
Daipung Monastery	Ming	Lhasa, Tibet	
Sera Monastery	Ming	Lhasa, Tibet	
Imperial Archives	Ming	Beijing	
Xuankong Temple	Ming	Hunyuan, Shanxi	
Tianyige Hall	Ming to Qing	Ningbo, Zhejiang	
Ancient Observatory	Ming to Qing	Beijing	
Zhenwu Hall at Jingluetai	Ming	Rongxian, Guangxi	
Qutan Temple	Ming	Ledu, Qinghai	
City Wall Tower	Ming	Southeast Part of Beijing	
Dujiangyan Irrigation Works	Qin to Qing	Guanxian, Sichuan	
Waterborne Penglai City and Penglai Hall	Ming	Penglai, Shandong	

Name	Period	Location	Remarks
Golden Hall at Great Harmony Palace	Qing	Kunming, Yunnan	
Yuyuan Garden	Ming to Qing	Shanghai	
Prince Gong's Residence and Garden	Qing	Beijing	
Wangshi Garden	Qing	Suzhou, Jiangsu	
Yongji Bridge at Chengyang	Republic of China	Sanjiang, Guangxi	
Labuleng Temple	Qing	Xiahe, Gansu	

(4) Stone Carvings and Others (2)

Name	Period	Location	Remarks
Iron Pillar	Song	Changde, Hunan	
Scripture Pillar at Temple to Soul-Saving Buddha	Kingdom of Dali (937-1094)	Kunming, Yunnan	

(5)   Ancient Sites   (10)

Name	Period	Location	Remarks
Yuanmou Man Site	Palaeolithic	Yuanmou, Yunnan	
Lantian Man Site	Palaeolithic	Lantian, Shaanxi	
Dawenkou	Neolithic	Tai'an, Shandong	
Hemudu	Neolithic	Yuyao, Zhejiang	
Zhouyuan	Western Zhou	Fufeng and Qishan, Shaanxi	
Site of Tonglushan Ancient Copper Mine	Zhou to Han	Daye, Hubei	
Ancient City at Wandushan	Korea (37 B.C.- A.D. 668)	Ji'an, Jilin	
Site of Hutian Ancient Porcelain Kiln	Five Dynasties to Ming	Jingdezhen, Jiangxi	
Ruins of Huining, upper capital of Jin	Jin	Acheng, Heilongjiang	
Ruins of the Imperial City of the Middle Capital and Stone Inscriptions at the Imperial Mausoleum	Ming	Fengyang, Anhui	

(6)   Ancient Tombs   (7)

Name	Period	Location	Remarks
Temple and Tomb of Sima Qian	Western Han to Song	Hancheng, Shaanxi	
Tomb of Yang Can	Song	Zunyi, Guizhou	
Song Mausoleum	Northern Song	Gongxian, Henan	
Tomb of Li Shizhen	Ming	Qichun, Hubei	
Tomb of Zheng Chenggong	Qing	Nan'an, Fujian	
Zhaoling Mausoleum	Qing	Shenyang, Liaoning	
Tomb of Genghis Khan	Rebuilt at a new site in 1954	Ejinhoro, Inner Mongolia	

Afterword

The State Council was being restructured when this booklet was in preparation. After the restructuring, some of the departments mentioned in this booklet have been merged or abolished.

1. The Ministry of Culture, the Commission for Cultural Relations with Foreign Countries, the State Administration of Publications, the State Bureau of Museums and Archaeological Materials and the Foreign Languages Publication and Distribution Bureau — formerly separate institutions directly under the State Council — have been combined under the jurisdiction of the Ministry of Culture. The State Administration of Publications is now the Administrative Bureau of Publications, while the State Bureau of Museums and Archaeological Materials is now the Bureau of Museums and Archaeological Materials.

2. The Central Broadcasting Administrative Bureau has been abolished and a new Ministry of Radio and Television has been set up.

文 化 事 业

《中国手册》编辑委员会编

*

外文出版社出版

（中国北京百万庄路24号）

外文印刷厂印刷

中国国际书店发行

（北京399信箱）

1982年（32开）第一版

编号：（英）17050—163

00115

17—E—1663P